To

G

and a great friend.

With love

Anna xx

Struck

Anna Saunders was born in Hoylake, Wirral and now lives in Cheltenham, Gloucestershire. Anna is Executive Director, and founder, of Cheltenham Poetry Festival and also works as a teacher and writing mentor. Anna is also the author of ***Communion*** (Wild Conversations Press) which was praised for its 'lush imagery and music' by Nigel McLoughlin. Anna's work has been published in journals and anthologies which include *Ambit, The North* and *Amaryllis*. She has recently completed a Masters in Creative and Critical Writing at The University of Gloucestershire.

Struck

Anna Saunders

Pindrop Press

Published 2014 by
P_indrop Press
Mallards
Steers Place
Hadlow
Kent

www.pindroppress.com

ISBN 978-0-9573290-5-8

A catalogue record for this book is available from the British Library.

Typeset by P_indrop Press.

Printed and bound in the UK by Lightning Source.

Cover image: *Quist Celeste* by Adam White
(http://www.adamwhiteartist.co.uk)

Acknowledgements

I should like to express my thanks to the editors of the following publications in which some of these poems appeared (or will appear shortly after *Struck* goes to press): *Ambit, Accente, Amaryllis, The Museum Of Light, The North, The Wenlock Poetry Festival Anthology 2014*.

My thanks also to: Nigel McLoughlin for his guidance and invaluable editorial advice; to my editor, Jo Hemmant; to David Clarke, Robin Gilbert and Jean Riley for their creative input and to my supportive and inspiring friends, family and fellow artists and writers.

for Peter Saunders

Contents

1 Birch

She traces his spine with a hot finger,
calls it a *sapling,*
says his metatarsal bones
resemble raised roots.

He finds heart-shaped leaves
with double teeth
flattened in a drawer,
last year's gold leaves
latticed in lingerie.

She scrutinises sharp buds
on slender shoots,
smoothes dangling catkins
between finger and thumb.

He catches her licking sap
surreptitiously,
stripping sheet-white bark
in a slow reveal.

She weeps at the idea
of lumber and pulp,
learns in Latin
Betula pendula.

He rips the axe
from the stump,
wipes the blade clean.

The Furies Tell Psyche She Sleeps with a Snake

its maw, weeping,
slipping across silk,
slick as an eel over ice.

They say he is serpentine.
Is seen submerged in a river
washing off her scent.

They say that he will eat her
when she is off-guard.

What girl doesn't trust her sisters?
So she holds up a torch as he sleeps
but sees only Cupid.

Cupid – young, wanton and lithe,
hairs on his limbs
iridescent as shafts of light.

No reptile leaking annihilation
or encased in scales – instead
only Cupid, son of Mars.

The Love God,
whose landed arrows
leave open wounds.

Cupid – bough-beaded with blood
and sleeping.

Summoning up energy
for his nocturnal flight.

Silks

If she could only forget
the way he slithered

belly down, rippling,
as if the earth were using him
for an accordion.

If she could see him instead
as a thing to inspire silks.

He claims he hasn't always worn
this viscous shell.
Suckled on soil
or cowered lowly.

He said all she need do is stroke him
and he will rise.

He flicks chiffon to peak and plummet.
Beats the air
with pearl-speckled gauze.
Twists sheets into a sheath,
enfolds them.

When she sleeps she dreams of pupae.
Embryos of men
breaking membranes to birth limbs,
thoraxes twitching
with unfurled wings.

She wakes foetal-trussed,
fingers spored.

Sees a collapsed silk shell.
His pearlescent signature
scribbled
from wall to door.

Xerxes' Defence

Brown as braised meat, truffle dark.
I lingered, who could blame me?

Beauty halts the hand.
I heard of a sunset once
stopped an army in its tracks.

Look how easily bark peels,
like lace from skin, how the leaves
shimmy like dancers' skirts.

I stripped my concubine's wrists,
hung her jewels. Bronzed baubles
bulbous as chestnuts, trailing catkins
of silver dangled from the boughs.

I watched stippled light quiver on bark,
and we were dappled, as if made of gold,
our skin broken to reveal it.

Its beauty bought my enemy
moments in the sun.

Dying men twitch and tremble.
A tree holds firm, casts a bold shadow.
May nothing shatter its sweet peace.

King Xerxes fell in love with an Oriental Plane tree, under which he paused, before marching on to war.

Palimpsest

We work through the winter
as snow blanks the land,
slay a whole herd for soft hides.

Velvet to vellum, beast to book,
he who hacks has God in his hands.

When there are no more calves to kill,
we wash the old books,
cleanse their claims with oats and milk,
prepare the page for the good word.

Occasionally a dark scribble
shows through, a drowned spider
rising to the surface of a lake.

As we work, serfs cross the fields.
They do not look behind as they approach.

They do not see the black earth birthed
by new steps in the snow.

The Waggish Musician

I was a human shield,
buffered his body with mine.

After they had fled he muttered
into my ear, sparking words
that made a glitter tide.

He'd caught the ear of the wolf first.
She'd nibble-groomed him
to his roots. He wedged her in oak
when he sickened of her.

Fox tempted him
with a slink of russet,
flashed her pelt like a flame.
He hung her in willow afterwards.

The hare's long ears were yielding,
easily flattened against her neck.
It was like re-corking wine,
using a rock to stop the burrow.

He came upon me whittling,
praised me for cutting the pale husk,
played me a song until the others
came running; hysterical creatures
who had bitten through their binds.
I wouldn't let them near him.

His touch was rough, rope-burnt.
When I woke I wondered
if I had imagined it.

How to Remove the Mandrake Root

Belladonna's sister
can make the barren bloom
like glass.
Be careful how you harvest it.

Do not pluck it from the peduncles
which spring from the neck
or try to pull it out
with your pale hand.

Instead bind a starved dog
to its base,
tempt it with a butcher's bone.

When it runs at you
it will rip the *love plant*
clean from earth.

If your dog freezes in fear,
draw three concentric circles
around the root.

Cut with your face toward the west,
speaking all you can
of the mysteries of love –

how it mutes the nerves of pain,
can cause madness.

The death song is a scream.
Plug your ears tight
as the sound can kill.

Avert your eyes from what remains –
a taupe lump resembling
both rough root
and coarse version of man.

2 The Butterflies Enter Our Rooms

Red Admirals pour through the letterbox,
wing-metals glittering like scratch cards.

An upstairs window is a mouth
for a flurry of papery tongues.

In the kitchen an Orange Tip hunts
for cuckoo flowers.
A Peacock circles the sink.

The room turns to a wind farm,
the air coursing our faces,

paperwork lifting off the shelves
as if it had wings.

Soon the ceiling is obscured
by a kaleidoscope of shifting scales.

We chase them out, secure the windows,
brush out the borders of the house.

Lie down in airtight rooms
dizzy with colour,
listening out for a beating of wings.

Columbidae

She comes clucking
in slate-grey suit,
muttering about the necessity for a cull.

I do not call them vermin
or wish them gone.

Consider the beauty of the birds,
I say.

See feathers loured like storm,
wings dark as smoke
rising from wet wood.

I leave food out.
Rain-bloated bread,
biscuits smashed to crumbs.

She accuses me of *courting* them.

The word for what those men were
is longer now.

It was a blunt noun
I scratched on a wall
before scampering away.

I can still feel their fingers
light as feathers. Ticklish.

Trauma tightens like a tourniquet.

I would not wish to be rid.
Their white scream
sticks the flakes of plaster,
holds my house together.

Sub Song

('All song is essentially sexual' – The Dictionary of Birds)

From beneath the canopy of Pyracantha
the blackbird's Sub song.

Male bird, occult
in the depth of hedge,

quivering larynx in a closed beak,
a pearl reverberating in a sealed shell.

This is not to be broadcast yet.
It is merely a warble,
a whisper song.

Rehearsal of the benign notes
that comprise its song.

The chuck chuck
scratchy staccato
rattle
of an overt call.

The male bird
orchestrating each utterance
under the still batons
of the boughs.

Like a lover, alone, in the night,
burrowing into bed,
muting his words in quilting,

going over each mellifluous line
until pitch perfect.

The lover alone, in the dark
preparing his fluty song,

rolling the notes in his mouth
until he softens the sudden
harsh chuckle
that always breaks out at the end.

Swift

When they needle her she is flying
and dreams on the wing
of rooftops glazed with rain,
spires the size of pinpricks.

When she wakes
there are small black birds
flitting under the eaves
and an inmate
flailing his arms as if in flight.

When will there be rest?
Her careering thoughts
dart and circle
like birds which will not land.

When they tell her she will be sectioned,
she shrieks, as above the asylum
the birds form a black gyroscope
which screams as it wheels.

An assault on the ears,
the nurse says,
injects her with something
to bring her back down.

Black arrows
melded to the bow
scratch the sky.

The devil's bird,
spits the nurse,
disturbed by frenzy.

Swallowing Starlings

Stand here, stare upwards
at what look like iron filings
or a locus storm.

Take a gulp of wolf sky
and swallow.

Resist the reflex –
the feathers in your throat
will thrash, the hackles rise
as gurgling they go down.

A conflicted flock
jostling each other to
pick the pulp from your skin
and leave you shot-peppered.

There are birds enough
to blot out the sun
and they will imitate darkness
as they nestle in your boughs,

but look closer
see the emerald in the wing,
the snowbird prophesy
of the white.

One day you will thrill
with the clamour
as they eat at you, will

blame the black
on the snapped end of a pen,

will seek out others
whose ecstatic song
of siren, whistle, squeak
echoes yours.

Prey

It is light when he lifts it,
like balsa wood.
His arms leap up, surprised.

At dawn, fleshy hillocks
warp the road.

He's seen splayed swans
that have mistaken
a motorway for lake.

Had owls flying at him,
ghosted by headlights,
luminous as angels
descending to earth.

The hawk's still flapping,
as he scoops it.

We are in their flight path,
he will explain in the morning
as he hands in his keys.

There won't be a mark
by midday, those
fluffy clumps
pestled into black
by other wheels.

3 White Hart

The room is lurid with moonlight
as he wakes to the staccato
call of owls, the sound of water,

his wife entering the room
squeezing her belly
as if it were a blister,
saying *I have lost it.*

All those months handling her
like she were a pitcher of juice
with no lid. Holding her up
to stop her spilling.

He takes to walking in the woods
at dusk. Sees the white hart,
luminous as a spirit
rising above the bracken.

Comes home, claims it moved
through the furze
as if it were immaterial.

Dreams of those flanks.
The sentience in its eyes.
The gentle way it chewed the cud.

Can't believe the rumours
at first of road-kill so big
they have to drive around it.

Goes out in the night
to see flanks smashed
like broken wings,

something seeping out,
meeting with the rain,

rushing off into the ruts
at the side of the pitted road.

Hung Game

In the painting
a dead partridge hangs
ripening its flesh.

Satin draperies billow
above a scarlet throne,
cotton peaks
on a mussed-up bed.

Underneath the *Game,*
a cat claws.

Skimpy feathers fall
as the cat swipes,
and the bird swings on one limb,
face obscured,
ankle lacerated by a ring.

The cat orbits the prey
as if gravitational forces
impelled it.

Hanging makes it easier to pluck,
you say.

Last night I thrust my wrists
towards you
like a jerked puppet.

You kicked ripped silk,
uncoiled a length of rope and said,
Let me.

The Knock

He doesn't dream of this
at school, before start of play,
his mind landing lightly
on each leaf of thought,
fluttering at the idea of *writing.*

His first job, to quiz
the parents of a son
who lies toe-tagged
in a drawer.

The father's fingers latticing
a crumpled face.
The mother fumbling
with the catches of a frame.

The obit will mention a love
of sport, include a picture
of a boy with a shy smile.

The pitch is platinum.
White-limbed, he radiates light.
As the ball soars,
he leaps for it, as if chasing the sun.

Closing-down Call

For days,
policemen turn the soil
like birds.

The evening before
he watches, mesmerised,
as a blue tit hops
round on a bough.

The killing comes
in the early hours,
with a cry like the hard call
of a crow.

But first, dusk,
and a flutter of wings so black
they could be an artist's impression
of night sky,
the blackbird's closing-down call.

Beach Combing

With fingers slim as razor shells,
he rakes detritus on the shore,

peels cloying strips of weed
from sand, lifts stones,

stirs a ripple in brackish waters
as white-bellied crabs scuttle.

In broken English, tells the air
how flotsam travels miles from wreck.
How the beached junk holds riches.

Last night the sea smashed a boat
its cargo of toys spilt and scattered.

Now flimsy plastic babies lie abandoned
across hard ridges of sea-stripped sand.

Tonight he will curl
foetal, as rain creeps up his clothes

and he will dream of hollow dolls
bobbing on black water,
tossed adrift and far from shore.

After Dinner

Someone switches on the light
and we float like life buoys
in the black lake of the glass.

How ebullient we are
with sugar rush,

bone-plucked by indolence,
jellyfish bells
quivering on the floor.

You are slick as a host,
your liniment-smooth hand
flush with mine.
Your voice planed to a polish.

Stories ascend from your lips
of Sue, who came home to a husband
crotch bulging in *Victoria's Secret*

and Mary,
waiting to have her sister
removed from her womb.

Thirty years old with her sister
hidden inside her
like a layer of a Russian Doll.

Inert and stunted,
only eight inches long.

Replete with hair and teeth,
adult teeth.

Another guest snorts,
Hairy Mary, he says.
Bucks his teeth out.
Makes like a rabbit.

We are still laughing
as Mary enters the room.
Imagine if that were your sister, she says.

In the black glass
of the window
my reflection bobs
like a bloated corpse.

4 Sugar, Symphony, Seductive

The silver birches fizz white
like an illustration of electricity.

She is squinting at her book,
eking out the last of the light.

For so long synapses have been firing
in him, sudden as a tripped switch.

He hates the way she says her s's.

Sugar, symphony, seductive.

Pages flutter like supplicating hands
as he knocks the book from her grasp.

Shambolic, sneaky, skuzzy.

White-winged flight peaks, plunges.
Ends face-down at his feet.

Savage, separate, schizophrenic.

The trees are aroused ghosts, hissing.

After Poetry

You crack the spine
of a new book. The author
is a realist, rages against romanticism
in a poem called *Fuck the Moon.*

You have to face facts,
you say, passing me my coat
just as gleaming white,
the moon emerges,
pale as a scallop shell
scooping out the dark.

The book eclipses
your face, as you read about
meat and gristle,

fingers splayed
on the black cover,
wedding band
conspicuous as Orion.

Cradling like Theo

After the overdose
I cradle your head
in the crook of my arm
in the same way Theo held Vincent.

The light is off.
Desperate for a way out
a crane fly batters against glass.

Your corn-pale fingers
twitch and stiffen.
Your eye-lids flutter
veined wings.

The only colour in the room
comes from acrylics.

Chrome-yellow
sears ultramarine skies.
Trees torch red ochre,
embered to black.

Vincent went to the Wheatfield,
planted a bullet in his heart.

You amputated the phone,
took twenty times
the maximum dose.

The sadness never ends
is what Vincent said.

The insect skitters
against a window
it has mistaken for sky.

It's black limbs flail
as if painting *impasto.*

The Memory of Muscle

Improvisation in the dance class,
they truss a woman up.

Five of them, looping nooses
over wrists and feet,
jerking the line back, taut.

Manacling the tips of her in strips
of sheets which still smell
of soap powder and *Comfort.*

Once she is in harness, she is made to walk.
It is arduous; her veins are up like girders.

Her cargo holds firm behind,
ball and chain shackling each step.

Now, she is told,
See what your body remembers.

The sheets are released.
For a moment she falls forward,
then seems to snap back.

Again, the slow agonized route
across the room. Her torso reigned
by an absent force.

Hours later, after the class, she wonders
why she walked as if she was still tied.

Takes to bed with the letter
he wrote her before he left.

On the edge of sleep,
her muscles contract
and her knees bend up in front of her

before her spine coils up concave,
as if to cup an invisible form.

In the Office

In white shirt, his torso
is camouflaged
against the bare walls.

His trousers have knife-
sharp creases, his polished shoes gleam.

He has a bullet-pointed list
which begins with Anxiety
descends through Depression,
Depersonalization
to Hyper-vigilance.

There is a footnote
about the dream in which he
places his neck on the track.

The list looks like a concrete poem
with an appendix.

Your brain is like a walnut
but more excessively folded,
the doctor says.

He shaved close
that morning, with a blunt blade.

Under a laundered collar,
blood blooms
like an atomic cloud.

5 **Honey**

All night he burrowed
as if she were an over-ripe apple.

His downy limbs
stealing her scent,
snaffling her sugar.

His mouth fixed fast
and suckling.

How honeyed his voice
afterwards
saying he would have *to fly.*
It still stung.

He had gorged.
Rocked back, bulging,
slug-drunk and drowsy

barb-blunted,
drugged and stumbling.

She watches him sleeping,
grips the heel of a shoe.

Thinks how easily
she could bring it down,
and with a quick swipe,
finish him.

Under Skin

Thou shalt not
necklaces his throat in *Helvetica,*
the sin is obscured.

He rolls a sleeve to show
Virgin Mary on his biceps,
her pious face pulvinated
with flesh.

He has a new one,
a pencil on the inside
of his thigh, a thick shaft,
bulging with fresh ink
where the skin is most silky.

You could do it,
if you keep your hands steady,
he says.

The words prick her epidermis
and amass, blood-hot,
rush to the surface
like a ripe bruise or blush.

Bait

She has caught his plump lip
and hooked it to a pout.

Oh, oh, oh.
Bubbles rise like hollow orbs
with each mute mouthing.

Not for the beauty of the bait
does he bob there.

Not for the beauty of the bait
or the way she loads the hook, heavily.

Nor for the morsel of flesh she dangles
pink as a shrimp,
plump as a maggot.

He comes for her soft cries
at each bite, the opaque petals
that blossom as she awaits
the twitch of line,

for the way she moans
at the taut pull
each time it plucks at her.

Gift

He twists the body.
Pushes it down, face first
onto a thin white sheet.

The page is pricked
before a fine character shows.

Faux gold, glint of gilt.
Nib brittle as crystal.

Slipped back into its box,
skinny corpse
into a soft coffin.

Thin rod,
spare as wishbone.
Sharp with purpose.

He offers her the box,
says, *our artefact.*
The polished words are piercing.

6 Flicking Switches and Lighting Candles

Was it worth it, that look?
Now the whites of her eyes are extinguished
like eggs tossed into a well.

He was beautiful,
sleek body a love letter
slipped under the door.

Now she is falling, like Eurydice,
into darkness. Pit-black,
rising like a night sea.

She buys bulb after bulb.
Forty watts then sixty.

At a hundred, worries if the heat
will eat holes in her shades
so she strips them.

Lets the nude bulbs bristle
hot and bare.

Spends all night
flicking switches
and lighting candles.

Wonders how she will cope
when winter comes.

The Kiss
After Klimt

He has the hands of a sensualist,
earth-brown,
stained as if scrumping plums.

She has scarlet peonies in her cheek,
a look of rapture. Purple blooms
rise through her dress, like dust
from a hot road.

They embrace on the edge
of a bed, or a cliff.

A slipped halo radiates
around them, unstable
as mercury dropped in a fire.

The dun sky has no stars
yet she is illuminated.

Inside his body are hard blocks
over which love streams
yet leaves unaltered.

In Limbo

In the gallery, a sky
purged of cloud
casts colour on a frozen lake.

Above ice, two girls float
cocooned in pale silk,

blond hair snagging
on claws of birch.

Two voluptuous pupae
hooked into suspension
between earth and sky.

Above their bodies
light strokes
resembling plumes of smoke.

That night,
strung up by insomnia,

she twists white sheets
into a sheath, wonders why
he hasn't called.

Sees again those women
plucked from time,
eyes closed tight
to seal in their dream.

Sees those wispy strokes
rising,

ascending ghosts
desperate
to be free of flesh.

Over the Roofs like Chagall

Curled foetal
he dreams he grips her,

ascends from the city,
rises on a sky which erupts
with plumes of fire and flower.

Morphs to one sinuous form
as they slither up towards angels

and blue cows tumble, flip,
and fish leer.

The *White-Winged* asking each other
if this is adoration
or abduction
or both –

as their heads break wings
like bright pollen stems
bursting through stargazers

and he looks down on that lank form,
her eyes closed as if in ecstasy,
as if in death.

Entering like Zeus

He is suggestive with colours
for the skin, dips blue in white
to evoke the marbled moon,

takes vermillion to her cheeks,
bleeds it to a blush,
opens her mouth with white.

With each stroke, he swells the flesh,
legs which were lean as wood
become sumptuously furnished.

When they call it *explicit,*
he will claim her legs are raised
in the tradition of Titian,

will lay the glittering myth
of Danae over her,
like gilt applied to a frame.

She thinks it is sunshine
that seeps through, quivering,
but that which creeps in

and runs through her
is a glittering rain
as hard and cold as coins.

The Old Man and Death

Light rakes twigs that tangle
like a viper's nest.

Last night you called on him
to release you from the endless cycle
of chop and stack,
the recurring birth of morning
and the darkness seeping in.

But when he comes
you can count his ribs,
calculate the cost of escape
in each linear slat of frame.

There he is before you,
leaner than the twigs
you have whittled.

You are close enough
to thread your fingers
through him, see them emerge
the other side.

Not yet. You drop your axe.
grind back down on rock,

drive your feet into earth,
whiten your knuckles
to the colour of moon.

Cyane's Testimony

The earth breaks open
and a mane, twisted
as sea weed, emerges.

A horse, eyes wild and white,
a creature bridled
in the heat of fear.

Four more stallions
burst through the core,
a cart bearing Hades,
shaking water from his cloak.

As I implore him,
his fingers press petals
into her skin.

Limbs scissor water.
Persephone hurtles
into the wound.

Bones, like hollow timber,
float in my pooling skin.

The stream's a sleeping draft,
I dream of fields of stunted corn,

wake to a mother's scream,
winter crossing the fields
fast as forest fire.

Diving

Inconsolable afterwards,
he buries his face
in a strip of furred sky
starred with sand crystals
scented with sweat, the sea and *Dior.*

His weeping vision
turning the cove
to a glazed dissolve,

shattering its smooth
surfaces into a disintegrated
form like fruit broken down
to a slick glitter.

In the chaos
he clings to his last sight of her
poised on the cliff,
ready to dive.

Afterwards, he has it in for the sea,
its smug murmur
and self-congratulatory applause.

Meets the waves
spit for spit, seethes
with each saline rasp
on shingle.

She comes floating to him
in dreams,
airborne, ascending.

With sleep's salt
beading his eyes,
he stumbles to the beach,

dives,

knowing she is too ephemeral
to be under earth

and instead is weightless,
gliding with angel fish
as if flying.

7 Poppy to Orchid

Holy red like prayer flags
rustling, paper light,
ruffle poised on stalk.

Dried to a pod.
Sliced to a sly eye,
opium weeps.

Scarlet burnt to brown.

Crystals shot through steel.
A surge through the stem
like sap.

The rush.
Skin splitting
to a wound.

Incubation.
Skin burns,
blues.

Pale petals
cluster a blood-bled stalk.

Orchids flower on an arm.

Written on Sand

Spume sizzles
like the dying bubbles
of spilt champagne
as your finger drives
through sand, draws a line
to separate past and present.

As the tide creeps in,
you say, *write all you desire*
in front of the line.
All you wish to forget,
behind the line.

I shape hard verbs
with clefts and hollows.

Words crumble
with soft mounds of
swept-aside sand.

We step back
as the tide, hissing
with sibilance,

licks the sand at our feet,
and with a quick flick
wipes out the line
separating past and present.

All Your Pet Names for Her

The day you leave, I interrogate you
about the euphemisms.

I get *Brown Sugar,*
have seen it on the spoon –
the colour of overturned earth,
clean of roots, dark
with the dirt of impurities.

And *smack,* a sweet, slick violence.
The tingle sting of a flat hand.

But *Horse*?
Is it because you buck and rear at night,
waking with white knuckles
over-thrown?

We didn't live in squalor, you say,
and I see you locking the door,
flicking switches,
running a rasping length of sulphur to pearl.

In the gloom, as white shrouds shudder,
you tighten a tourniquet
until electric blue lightning forks ascend

and then you slip her under your skin,
eyes rolling up to the ceiling
as if you could see angels there, grappling.

Autopsy of an Old Passion

After Dan Burt

Imagine you are slicing an envelope
just wide enough to peek inside.

Weigh up whether the fault is
overwork, or inactivity.

Was the blood swift, or sluggish?
Did the heart miss a beat, or barely drum?

Try to focus, this is an enquiry
into what can be done
to keep the next one alive.

Future treatments may include
oysters, silks, candlelight, torch songs.

Don't get distracted by the mouth.
Only an amateur would imagine
that, after all this time,
her lips could still have the power
to breath life back in.

8 What's the Time, Mr Wolf?

Anything can be an 'in',
a giggle, a request for the time.

Easy to act giddy
up here, as if from altitude –

the bar stool the pinnacle
to an arduous ascent
in kitten heels.

Sometimes the scar
sparks things off,
Do you remember the game?

A high sun casting small shadows,
the shrill question, then retort,

One o'clock, two o'clock!

Small paces are best,
a short distance traversed
that can be regained, easily.
Dinner time!

Running a little slower
so you can get caught.

The grapple and fall,
slow leak of blood and tears.

Twenty years later
the stitches still show.

Invariably
they will trace the indentation
in your knee
and allude to it later,
telling you it doesn't detract
from your looks

and, if they do leave you sleeping
in a scooped-out bed,
you still have the word *beautiful,*
to nestle like a candy
in your mouth

until you have extracted
all of the sweetness
and the compliment crumbles
upon your tongue.

The Rack

As you comb the knots
from my pillow-mussed hair,
we watch 'the girl raised by wolves'
learn to crawl.

First, she scampers across the screen,
scuttles quickly out of sight
then is brought back,
positioned in front of the camera
and made to walk.

As she executes each stumbling step,
her legs judder and wobble
and her back dips.

It's as if she has no spine,
you say, and switch off
as the girl is being made to hang
off a rack.

With steel teeth,
you tear apart a kink
and I stand passive
as a horse in harness.

All the time I'm thinking
of wolf girl
sweating under strip lights,

of the white teeth,
of the nurses' grins.
The light glinting on the metal rack.

You Were Born with Six Legs

A wave sucks back the shore of now
and the hospital recedes. He is back
on the terrace, the voice of Joan, his PA,
surging over him, sibilant-soft.
Ssh, she says as he swears.
The cocktail comes in sugar-rimmed
glass, mint-leaf garnish a crown of thorns.
You were born to a sow, he says, smiling,
as she scoops up black olives, the oil
glistening on her chin. There's a corker
of a sunset starting. The Stroke Ward
looks out over a car park. Gulls
who have no memory of the sea
tear at black plastic, scavenge in bins.
Lovely shoes Joan, are they Italian?
The sky's core is platinum,
mottled with peach. Joan will get his jacket
when it gets chilly. He couldn't have done
without her when his wife died.
They feed him cold potatoes,
almost liquid but with lumps.
The sky is maroon, veined with scarlet
and glistens like marble. They love
the scent of the sea. There's nothing like it,
except perhaps the wild garlic
with the tiny white stars they saw in the woods.
The nurse lifts the cup up to his lips,
spills some. *You were born with six legs*, he says.
As she wipes it off him, he waits for a smile
that doesn't come. The gold is gone, lilac is deepening to black.

There Is Always the Dance

On the way home, body
buoyant on water,
lithe tide holds him aloft.

Days before, the sea's quicksilver
shimmy, caprice of cirrus
in an improvised sky.

Dust motes had danced for him.
A fly hummed to the drum
in the pulse.

A poor translation of a smile,
he is sentenced in a second.
Two men execute their intent
with fists like full stops.

Un-choreographed clouds collide,
bulk against brawn as they beat him.

Silk-strung, the tree sings of him.
His legs kick out as if at a ceilidh.

Multani Mitti

She sleeps as if her mind were swathed
in khaki, dun dreams; dusty with earth and ashes.

When she wakes she remembers
how, after smoking something filthy,
her son had knocked that girl to the ground.

15 years old and on her way home after looting,
arms full of over-ripe apples, toilet tissue and tins.

Out there a month, he'd already seen bloated bodies
bob like sick fish on the surface of rivers,
his own men blown Jack–in-the-box
through the tops of jeeps.

Once, home on leave,
he had bought her a silk scarf.

She'd been astonished at how its colour
matched the green in her eyes.

They May Last for a Few More Days

The radio speaks of more troops sent out.

By December another ten thousand men may be deployed

Emptying the water from the lilies,
she peals a lank, rotting leaf,
plucks a dead-head.
Already the civilian cost is immeasurable
Pink-tipped Stargazers
bought earlier in the week
and already past their best.

The count is now perhaps running to thousands
Their fragrance heady as incense
even now as the petals fall.
And reports are coming in of an attack on a mosque
Lowering her head,
the scent assails her,
Witnesses say a solider threw a grenade in to a mosque

and the ochre pollen stains.
killing a congregation of mainly women, and children

As she lifts her head she is startled
to see a dark patch
on the side of her face.

Blotched as a burn.
Mottled as the colours of khaki.

Revolutionary Road

The station wagon gasps against gravel,
and Jack stops in his tracks
at the sight of April,
maroon-faced, driving the mower
across an unforgiving
lawn, eyes hard as the stone
at the heart of a peach.

Later, Jack nurses scuffed knuckles,
Alice washes the wall
free of blood.

Then they are in bed
and he is thinking
how murky the moonlight is
compared to her skin.

Tomorrow there will be a row
over groceries. Someone
will have bought the wrong brand.

He will notice
how her posture slumps.
She will see a paunch
bulge over his jeans.

But for now they have
that tangle of limbs.

Her voice running over him
like a river
and him glistening and wriggling
in it, like a minnow in sun.

Immersion Therapy

This isn't as overt as spiders
dropped through a hatch,
threads trailing the cheeks
in a furred scratch and tease.

Or the sound of a dog's staccato
bark played on a loop. Or being dangled
over the sea, shoved into a pen of wolves.

It isn't as direct as being suspended
in a trunk while wasps
rage around you like aural furze.

This is a treatment for *doxophobia* –
you fear being bear-marauded
if honeyed with language.

You suspect the colour of compliments.
Worry that a hammer blow of affection
will tenderise you like meat on a slab.

The cure involves enclosure,
a slow, measured exposure,
the source of discomfort
to be sealed away.

All those adjectives,
inspired but unspoken,
confined in the box, a blindfold
wrapped around the eyes.

If there is no adverse reaction,
the lid may be lifted,
the words let out, one by one,
gradually amassing
to a pool of liquid gold.

The result is dazzling,

and the subject blinks and blears
covers his eyes,

and, like a mole emerging from soil,
drags his weight into the light.

9 Struck

Walking together for the first time,
our path is crossed by a tree
downed by lightning.

Charred and toppled,
lying spent, boughs frozen
in the act of grasping,

one tree struck
amongst countless
upstanding trunks.

How sudden the hit,
easy to miss
the first trailers
drawing a route for the bolt.

Pre-emptive strikes
whose sketched path
arouses a tremor
like a finger
swooping down the spine.

Quick silvers –
synapses shooting signals
from fingers to brain.

This is how you come undone,
the flicker
then hot bolt igniting the husk,
roots splitting like scorched stitches

until any hold on the earth is lost
and the whole torso tumbles
and falls.

Hunter Moon

Cirrus clouds sprawl
like crumbled clothes
dropped on night sky.
Hunter Moon flashes a bloom.

It has shimmied escape
from black silks,
is bald as a bulb,
bulging each milky curve
of its blue-blood body.

Last night you lay stripped
and still, skin pulsing,
limbs fizzing light

as my eyes bleared
at the curve and dip,
luminous and unearthly.

How the *other* enthrals us,
an alien splendour
ghosting the mind,

looming over sleep,
its iridescence almost too dazzling
to view.

Song

At midnight I open to your touch.

Muted moans
furnish the air like fabric.

I sleep coiled in on myself,
knotted as a root.

The space you leave
is furrowed.

At dawn, daffodils,
weak from severing
a carapace of bulb,
bow their heads
as if in penance.

The birds call out
in the hard dark,

their songs
soft tapestries
covering a stone floor.

At Sea

Sleep closes over your head like water
and your mouth pouts fish-like
as you mumble the tongue of dreams.

All night we take turns to be
an arc of wave rising,
the shore beneath

and we whisper
with surge and retreat,
our twisted limbs
slick-drizzled weeds clinging.

This is where love washes us up:
me, light as a boat, bobbing,
you throwing an anchor of limb.

Fireworks

We are too remote
to hear the strike of sulphur,
to watch a pole pushed
into pliant earth.
Your skin is already cooling.

Our reflections haunt black glass.
I circle the edges
of your light like a moth,
twitch at the shriek
and high-pitched whine of ascension.

Not a breath is spent.
Light spangles,
colour blossoms,
a flower under time-lapse photography.

It's as if it never happened
I say, and you talk about *burn out*
as the warm wax of your body goes cold.

You are already in the other room
when it begins again
and you miss the whisper then rising cry
before another explosion

even brighter than the last
makes its fleeting impression
upon a darkening sky.

10 The Sighting

My father's master class
in sitting still and observing
pays off one night

when a single point of light emerges
and then a second light,
a third, fourth, hovering apart
in perfect co-ordination
too slow for plane,
too high for helicopter.

Since the stroke he has
smelt beef at 2am,
seen dead cats dart under doors,

so he calls in his wife
to validate his vision
and they stand at the window,

the two of them
still as horses in a field,
flank to flank, slowly breathing,

standing so close it is as if
they were one.

I walk in on them,
catch a glimpse
of a dark form pulsing
with two hearts

before the seam
between them splits,
my father separates

and turns to me, smiling,
gesturing at something alien
yet still dazzling which lights up
the starless sky.

A Wind Fret

A wind fret, my father says.
I lower my ears to undercurrents,
his vocals are swarthy
as a saline-seasoned log.

High tide again, I hear him rasp.
Sometimes he props the bed
so he won't drown.

Earlier, light enough
to make your eyes weep.

Perched on a rock
to watch Snow Buntings
butterfly-twitch on the shore.

He warmed his bones until
an unannounced louring.

Remember once, we ran from one?
A black ball. Sick of being thrown,
rolling slowly towards us, across the shore.

We had taken our shoes in our hands.
Scarpered.

I picture him through the wash
of his words, a flinty figurehead
breaking the waves.

The sun's gone in, he says.
Suddenly, and without warning,
his lungs whimper
like something shot through, leaking air.

Butterfly Father

We did not love the pupae stage,
incubation of sickness,
you, swathed in off-white,
limbs bound to a wiggle,
caterpillar body breaking down
as we watched over you, each moment
bringing some subtle change.

You waited for us to leave
before you burst through falteringly,
shaking out shriven wings
like silk, beating down air
until you rose to the ceiling's paper moon,
shadow cleft as a heart,
kaleidoscope limbs emblazoned with eyes.

Into the Box

Ladies and gentlemen,
do not let your attention stray
for a second.

Observe, if you will,
the familiar creature
scuffling a little, on the spot.

Watch the pink nose twitching,
abdomen billowing
with slow breath.

See how oblivious he is
to what comes next.

One minute, the breath,
the body billowing,
the lowering into a box,

a black cape eclipsing the cage
like a dead star before the sun.

You blinked, missed it.
I bet you wish you had warned him
how the darkness would feel.

Here's the trick –
the disappearance of solid mass.

Step forward.
Observe only the dust mites tumbling
the hollow box.

The empty space
you can put your hand through.

Registering the Death

In the basement window
weeds spiral and knot
like ferns in a tank.

They are sunk below the streets,
separated from sunshine
which hovers above, haloing soles.

The reeds ripple and swell
as the registrar scribbles
and a passing sequinned shoe
glints like a fin.

The desk is disordered
as a shipwreck
with rusty scissors, paper-clips,
a toppled cup.

A plimsoll paddles in a pool of light
and a dog's snout pushes
through the greens, grey as a seal.

As the registrar passes her the certificate,
she gulps for breath, fills her lungs,

readies herself to break surface
and join the shoal
that drifts over her head.

In the Clearing

I dreamt him in halo of fire,
I say. Describe
last days spent bedded down,
drawing nutrients
from the dark, emerging
in the morning as a weak shoot.

We stand by two dead trees,
one toppled, one upstanding,
boughs raised in exaltation.

It is pale as a sapling,
stripped limbs
contrast with the sky
like bone on blue silk.

Death has hollowed it.
The weightless timber
turned flute
for the wind
to blow oracle through.

In the afternoon light
it is luminescent,
an angel-blazing glory.

I remember thin hands,
veins raised as roots,
light blasting from eyes
like sun through stained glass.

My dying father standing there,
rustling down his wings.

Moth

She has kept almost all his clothes.
Sedate suits, blazers,
old school ties.

On the edge of tears
at the holes in a sweater,
she lifts up the furred patch
of navy blue
to make a strip in the sky.

Oh, oh, she moans.
Her mouth, an oval,
mirrors the gaps in wool.

The sweater is a night sky –
starless, dark,

peppered with the kind of holes
a husband could tumble through
as he fell off the face of the earth.

Where Are the Ghosts When You Want Them?

The girl in the 'Shock Flick'
startles when she hears
the groan of a ghost
dragging a stump
down the parquet floor.

Recoils
when she realises it is her uncle,
the one who *bought it*
when his brakes failed.

She doesn't want him back,
not like this, not as a bruise
on the air, a thickening
of the atmosphere.

Not see-through,
a dirty pearl chiffon
drifting over furniture
like a wind-blown blouse.

Some of us welcome the weightless.
Sit up all night
waiting for a door to dance.

Ears primed
for sounds of shuffling.
Eyes alert for the sight of grey.

Butterfly Father II

The impression is of a leaf rising,
but it's my butterfly father
on the other side of the glass.
This time he's black.

Beneath us, the buddleia teems
with the pages of dolls-house
books, white-leaf, blank.

Papilio Papa,
unwilling to leave the *dark art,*
wings gleaming like wet prints.

Black butterfly making a mark
in the clear sky. Wavering flight
the scribble of a trembling hand.

Testimonials

Struck is an intricate weave of images held before reality, its threads pulled together by a recurrent series of physical materials and ideas – birch, skin, writing, above all silk which describes the weave itself. There is too a sustained symbolism of colour – of brown and blue and grey – a symbolism which, though it never hangs heavy over the poems, is nevertheless strong enough to cope with the weightiest subjects: love, physical nature, violence and – in a powerful and lucid closing sequence about the poet's father – death. Not a single image or symbol is wasted or forgotten. What stays with you at the end is not so much the subjects or the myths the poems draw on – Danae, Zeus, Van Gogh, the figures from Chagall, compelling as those are, – as the astonishingly original and fresh technique of a poet of quite remarkable gifts.
Bernard O'Donoghue

The poems are passionate, acutely observed and strikingly original. They explore and discover original, surprising and truthful territories and dimensions of human feeling and experience, and are astoundingly alert to the complex and mysterious experience of being alive. A very fine, beautifully sustained collection by a gifted poet whose work is unfolding in remarkable directions.
Nick Drake

The figures in Anna Saunders' collection are struck by desire, betrayal, loss and grief. They inhabit a mythical landscape where women fall in love with trees, the dying are transformed into butterflies, and lovers are secretly serpents. Saunders' metaphorical language is rich yet exact, offering us opulent, yet precisely crafted miniatures of human beings at the extremes of emotional experience. This is a bold and beautiful collection which deserves a wide readership.
David Clarke, poet and author of *Gaud*, Flarestack

Struck is a wonderfully appropriate title for this collection. There is an extraordinary suddenness about the imagery in so many of the poems; a series of shocks of recognition when fundamental aspects of existence are fully experienced as if for the first time. The poet conveys moments of startling and painful clarity when forks of lightning pierce open the night sky. It is only when electric blue lightning forks ascend ('All Your Pet Names For Her') that one can be most acutely aware of the bewildering beauty and fragility of life. This book is rather like an Immersion Therapy for the reader where the result is "dazzling,/ and the subject blinks and blears/covers his eyes,/and like a mole emerging from soil/drags his weight into the light".

The series of poems about the death of the poet's father are particularly tender and moving where love and loss merge as the past and present merge: we are told in 'Written On Sand' that the line between them has been wiped out. You might say that these poems attempt the most difficult thing in life: to be fully aware of the fullness and mystery of the present moment.....so dazzling and intoxicating are the images in this collection that one feels on reaching the last page that one could echo the final words of the poet's father in 'A Wind Fret': "The sun's gone in".
James Knox Whittet. Award winning poet and author of ***When Kafka Met Einstein***

Anna Saunders' collection *Struck* is aptly named. I was struck by the balance between meditative and sensual, accepting and angry, but always beautifully observed poems. Grief, desire, mythology and modernity all balance in the energy with which she uses image, line music and breath. The voice is achieved and authentic, and builds beautifully across the different moods and themes of this collection. The work in ***Struck*** extends and deepens the achievement of her previous collection ***Communion***. This is a poet going from strength to strength.
Nigel McLoughlin, Professor of Creativity & Poetics, University of Gloucestershire

Anna Saunders' collection ***Struck*** fizzes with life and light. It marks the emergence of a powerful, assured and eloquent new voice, a voice that can rise to heights of clarity and conviction or drop to a seductive murmur; that can draw with equal skill contemporary language and the archetypes of mythology. If you're looking for poetry with a little extra excitement, allow yourself to be struck.
Ross Cogan, author of ***The Book I Never Wrote*** and ***Stalin's Desk***

Lightning Source UK Ltd.
Milton Keynes UK
UKOW03f1359070314

227753UK00001B/1/P

9 780957 329058

~ Sunday 21st June, 1925 ~

At last this voyage is nearly over! It hasn't been the most pleasant six days of my life; I've spent most of the trip confined to my cabin with a nasty case of *mal de mer*, but the last couple of days have been rather better and I am on deck enjoying the fresh sea air and in the mood for some social interaction.

I have so far avoided the company of my fellow passengers, partly because of my delicate state but also because I had packed a selection of improving books for the voyage and once I had sea-legs enough to enjoy them I spent many hours in my cabin reading. One is a volume on the archeology of the British Isles, which I am reading as preparation for the research I plan to engage in once settled in England; another is a quintessentially English Gothic novel, Emily Bronte's *Wuthering Heights*. There was also a book from my mother on British etiquette, which I've granted a cursory glance. I'm sure my English relatives will pardon the occasional *faux pas* from their American cousin!

This morning the weather was fine, a blue sky with a scattering of cloud and a gentle sea breeze. I elected to take my book on deck and made myself comfortable on a deckchair. As it was still early in the morning, most of the other passengers were still at breakfast so I would be undisturbed for an hour or so. I was interrupted from my study of Mortimer Wheeler's recent excavations by the sound of running feet and a voice crying "Hie! You stop, sir! Stop that man!"

A second later a man paused by my chair. He was not pleasant to look at, possessing a pallid and unshaven countenance topped by a battered white Panama hat. I noticed that his cream linen suit was extremely crumpled and bore many stains from the voyage.

He also, I'm afraid to say, exuded an unpleasant aroma not unlike rotten fish. The chap was breathing heavily and momentarily ducked down by the side of the chair, as if to conceal himself, before leaping up again and running a few yards down the deck before stopping suddenly, turning to run back the way he'd come then changing his mind and sprinting off in the direction of the lifeboats. All this just in time to evade one of the ship's officers, a somewhat rotund middle-aged gentleman who trotted, puffing and panting, in hot pursuit. It was he, obviously, who had requested that the miscreant should stop.

Finding his quarry had made good his escape, I was subjected to a short interview with the officer. Had I seen a stowaway? In which direction had he gone? I attempted to return to my book but my curiosity was piqued so I took a walk along the deck in the hope of seeing the conclusion of the episode. There was a splash and both I and my new companion rushed to the side of the ship only to see the man in the water and swimming away at a frantic pace. The officer expressed his intention to launch a lifeboat and haul the miscreant back aboard. Before this could be done, however, the man sank under the water leaving only his Panama hat floating on the surface as a make-shift grave marker. The naval officer was concerned for my welfare, I being a young lady who had just witnessed either an unfortunate accident or a deliberate suicide, but I am made of strong stuff and was more intrigued than alarmed by the incident. Reassured, the officer departed for his cabin doubtless to make his report in the Ship's Log. I resumed my reading only to be pleasantly interrupted by a steward bearing my morning tea and toast. Many other passengers were out and about now, unaware of the morning's excitement. I decided to join the crowds at the rails to catch a first glimpse of my mother's home country, England.

As I got up I saw a small thing glittering in the sunlight, right beside my chair. It was an odd figurine, only about four inches in height. Examining it further I could see that it was a beautifully crafted golden figure of a man with a fish's tail. How extraordinary!

The only people to have passed me that morning were the drowned man and the ship's officer. I guessed that it was the drowned man who had dropped it. I should have reported it to someone, I suppose, but there was something about the statue that drew me in. The best way to explain it is like when my grandmother gave me a family heirloom, a bracelet, as a twenty-first birthday present. I didn't have the slight discomfort that one gets with jewelery until one gets used to the weight; it felt like it had always been part of me. The statue felt the same. To give it up would have felt like giving up Grandma's bracelet. I felt a little guilty, but I slipped it into my bag. I reassured myself that its curiously light weight meant that it wasn't gold so it was probably a pretty trinket of little value.

We're due to dock in Southampton in less than an hour and my Aunt Mildred is to meet me there. Mother has decided that this gal has been mixing with some odd company back home; there was that strange incident in Maine that quite ruined a family vacation, I suppose. I am, therefore, to stay with her sister, Lady Mildred Ashwood, in her stately pile in Surrey in the vain hope that it will transform me.

I've wanted to visit England for a long time, to visit the British Museum and see the antiquities, but the only way I could afford it was if Mother paid, so I agreed. I'm not looking forward to seeing my cousin, Alice, again, though. She visited us some years ago and I found her to be a thoroughly spoiled little madam. She is eighteen now, so I'm sure she's matured – almost time to disembark. I must pack!

~ Later ~

I want to record every little detail in this journal as this may be the only time I visit the Old Country and I want to look back when I'm ninety and be able to recall every day just as it happened! If every day is like today, however, I'm not sure that resolve will last very long.

Aunt Mildred was indisposed so the welcome party consisted of Alice, my Aunt's maid, Bartram, and Grayson the chauffeur, a good-looking young chap who gave me a friendly wink as he loaded my trunk into the Bentley. Bartram appeared a bit of a sour puss and gave me a cursory greeting followed by one of those looks down her nose, before falling silent for the remainder of the journey.

Alice has turned out very pretty. My Aunt and my mother were similar in looks and Alice took after both of them being small, slender, blonde and blue eyed. I favor my father so there was little family resemblance. She welcomed me with a hug and spent the hour or so we were driving going over my itinerary for the following weeks. We would easily be home in time for dinner. Did I like duck? She and my Aunt had great plans for my stay. Tomorrow we would go into the West End and I could help her choose a new hat. She didn't ask me if I cared for hats. I do not particularly care for hats.

I said that I was keen to do some shopping but wondered if it might also be possible to take a little time to visit London's excellent museums. Alice was unimpressed. Why would I want to look at a lot of boring old stones when London was so much fun? I hated myself for thinking it, as Alice was trying her best, but goodness me she's going to be difficult to get along with! While a new frock or two would, of course, be the bee's knees, I was running short of reading material and there is more to life than being in the fashion!

I was quite relieved to finally arrive at the house, Boughton Court, a handsome square Georgian place surrounded by a beautifully kept garden. I met Aunt Millicent at dinner, along with my Uncle Thomas. He's a nice old buffer, as they say in Britain. See, I'm learning the local parlance already!

Uncle Thomas loves history too and we had a lovely chat about Roman mythology over the soup. Aunt Millicent interjected "Thomas, don't bore Neve with that nonsense!" so, by the duck and green peas we were back to hats, frocks and what is showing at the picture house. I will make an effort to seek out Uncle Thomas tomorrow after we return from shopping.

~ Monday 22nd June ~

Today has been quite remarkably tedious. Aunt Millicent had decided to prepare me for my introduction into London society so after breakfast she summoned the Bentley and she, Alice and I motored into town to augment my wardrobe with a few party frocks. We collapsed into the motor in the late afternoon laden with boxes and bags of all kinds; so many that the friendly chauffeur had a job to fit them all into the trunk.

The weather remained sunny and after being parked outdoors all day the car was very hot. As we drove back to Boughton Court, Aunt wound down the window and began to fan herself, complaining that she was feeling faint. Grayson pulled over and she hauled her not insubstantial personage out onto the grass verge. Alice twittered and fussed around her mother without actually helping the situation whilst I scrabbled around in my bag for the bottle of smelling salts I knew was in there somewhere. I located the small bottle and as I pulled it out something scratched my hand, badly enough to make it bleed. Alice called out to hurry up with the smelling salts so I pressed a clean handkerchief over the wound for a moment until the bleeding stopped then got on with playing nursemaid to Aunt Mildred, who was perfectly fine after she'd got some fresh air. The emergency over, we piled back into the car and the rest of the journey passed uneventfully. The remainder of the afternoon was spent watching Alice try on all her purchases – very dull.

In the evening, however, things became a little more interesting. My Aunt had invited a few of Alice's friends over for dinner, reassuring me that it was not a party but simply a gentle introduction to a few people nearer my age. I was surprised when Alice tapped on my door while I was dolling myself up for company. She stepped in almost timidly, in a manner quite unlike the carefree ebullience I was growing to expect from my cousin. She sat on the bed watching me do my hair.

"I wish I had beautiful green eyes like you, Neve," she said. "They're like limpid pools. I read that in a book. It's jolly poetic, don't you think?"

I laughed. "You have very pretty blue eyes, Alice. Everyone says so."

"I suppose you know that Daddy's friend is coming to dinner?" she went on, twisting a lock of hair between long, beautifully manicured fingers. "I hope Mummy doesn't make me sit next to Mr Albright. I don't like him much."

"I thought we were just expecting some friends of yours," I replied.

"We were but Daddy said as Mummy was entertaining he was sure one more wouldn't make much difference. He's an old chap, some kind of professor. He visits us sometimes to look at Daddy's Roman things. He's not very nice". She shuddered. "Still, Honoria and Bingo are just lovely and they're bringing a pal of Bingo's too. We might still have a spiffing time". She sighed and went off for her bath.

At a few minutes past eight a car horn honked noisily in the driveway and a motor car drew up and deposited three people at the door. The visitors were Alice's friends, a cheery dark-haired young woman called Honoria and her husband, who I'm sure has a proper name but everyone calls him Bingo, even Aunt Millicent. Accompanying them was Bingo's chum, Archie Glossop. Alice, Aunt Millicent and Honoria were soon swept up in much animated talk about Honoria planning a new garden for her and Bingo's lovely house in Hampstead while I was left to chat to the rather quieter Archie.

Archie had an open, freckled face and a beautifully tailored dinner jacket that didn't quite convince. What he lacked in elegance, however, he more than made up for in conversation. He and Bingo were old school pals and it was quite natural that they had shared a flat when both of them fetched up in London, before Bingo had married Honoria. He told me that Honoria has a job, which is unusual for a woman of her social class. She works in the Houses of Parliament, so that's all right, and it's ever so handy when Bingo's pater is sitting in The Lords.

Bingo does something or other in publishing (I gather that the English upper class think having an actual job is rather vulgar) while Archie is an academic, researching all manner of interesting things to do with Middle Eastern history. He is currently spending most of his time at the British Museum cataloging a quantity of artifacts from a dig in Iraq which date back to the days of ancient Mesopotamia and are particularly relevant to his research interests. They have been in the museum's stores for some years and Archie is anxious to finish the job so that more of them can go on display.

For the first time since I arrived in England I was feeling truly comfortable and happy.The conversation was fascinating and was only interrupted by the butler bearing a welcome glass of sherry.

My Aunt was looking anxiously at the clock. I could tell that she was worried about the food spoiling: it was some twenty minutes later than we had intended to sit down for dinner. I could tell she was relieved when the doorbell rang again. A gaunt figure entered the drawing-room a few moments later. It was a gentleman rather short in stature and I would estimate his age at around fifty. He came accompanied by a slightly musty odor, not unlike the smell of a public library. This was obviously the "professor" Alice disliked so much.

My Uncle had been disinclined to join in the chat about how hard it was to get a good gardener and had kindly not interrupted Archie and I. He became very animated, however, when this dinner guest entered the room, shaking his hand for some time and exclaiming "Welcome, welcome, old fellow!" he gestured for the man to sit down but my Aunt intervened by asking Bartram to sound the dinner gong.

I was seated with Archie on my left side and Mr Albright, my Uncle's special guest, on my right. I noted that my Aunt had placed herself on Albright's other side. Alice must have been relieved. The butler poured some wine and Bartram served the soup.

Social convention dictated that by dessert I should have curtailed my chat with Archie and begun a conversation with Mr Albright. Although Alice and I have little in common I agreed with her opinion that Albright was not pleasant company. Even when my Uncle greeted him so effusively the man had barely smiled. He did, however, cheer up a little when I asked polite questions about his field of study. He explained that he was not in fact a professor, as Alice thought, but was actually a dealer in antiquities and rare books. My Uncle is one of his best customers and the two have been friends for many years.

As he spoke, Albright leaned in towards me rather more than I liked. I could smell sour breath, stale tobacco and old books. He insisted that I used his first name – Ebenezer – and called me Neve, which I thought over-familiar given we had just been introduced.

Further, as we talked he felt the need to emphasize a point from time to time, which he did by putting his hand on my knee. This made me very uncomfortable and I wished he would stop, but I didn't want to make a fuss and risk offending my Uncle who obviously held the man in great regard.

Archie, bless him, noticed me squirming every time Albright positioned himself closer and thought it best to intervene.

"Mr Albright, I fear you are crowding Miss Selcibuc" he hissed.

Albright responded much more loudly. "I'll thank you to mind your own business, Glossop! I'm sure Neve and I are getting along famously!" This accompanied by another pat on the knee, but this time the man did not remove his hand.

Albright feigned a smile as he responded to Archie but his face betrayed his true feelings, clearly showing anger at the younger man's challenge. Conversation at the table stalled as Honoria and Bingo glanced first at their friend and then at Albright. Archie had flushed red and was also struggling to control his temper. His hands were balled into fists on the table. Aunt Millicent looked flustered and signaled to the butler to refresh everyone's glasses.

The rest of the meal passed in uncomfortable silence and I think all of us were relieved when Uncle Thomas and Albright took themselves off to the study with the bottle of whisky. My Aunt announced that she had a slight headache and was going to bed. Once she was safely out of the way Honoria, with a gleam of mischief in her eye, asked if the butler might fetch the gramophone. A few minutes later the furniture had been pushed back and *I Wish I Could Shimmy Like My Sister Kate* was on at full volume. Archie and Bingo improvised a ridiculous dance which quite restored the party's good humor, then Bingo took Honoria's hand and Archie mine and dragged us into the Charleston. Such fun!

"Well I'll say, Alice, this is absolutely the cat's pajamas!" I opined, forgetting that my mother said I must remember to talk like a lady. Alice laughed and ordered the butler to bring champagne.

I decided that I'd been too harsh in my initial judgment of my cousin. She was rather shallow, perhaps, but she was sweet and funny and she certainly knew how to throw a party. Her friends were adorable – naughty, bright Honoria, amiable Bingo and shy, earnest Archie! I hadn't expected to enjoy myself so much and was even able to forget the unpleasant episode with Albright for a while as we danced and danced, although I did refuse Honoria's offer of a cigarette.

Alice and I waved our guests off a little after midnight. As the butler bustled about with coats, I saw Bingo lean forward and murmur something in Honoria's ear. I caught her response. "Darling, there's no harm in it and Archie hasn't looked this happy since the wedding." I took this to mean Honoria and Bingo's recent matrimonials; Archie seemed like the kind of chap to take pleasure in his friends' happiness. Then car doors slammed, the engine revved and wheels crunched on gravel as my new chums sped off into the night.

It was then that I noticed there was still a light under my Uncle's study door. Alice hoped that Albright would not be staying the night; neither of us was keen to make his acquaintance again. Bartram appeared looking none too happy at having to work so late and started crashing bottles and glasses about in the dining room. Alice and I retired, but I couldn't settle immediately and sat reading for a while. The grandfather clock in the hallway struck 2am before I heard Albright's voice: "Goodnight, Sir Thomas". There were footsteps on the landing and the door of the room next to mine squeaked as it opened and closed. Suddenly stricken with a case of the heebie-jeebies, I leaped out of bed and turned the key to lock my door. Bartram would just have to knock loudly when she brought me my morning tea!

~ Tuesday 23rd June ~

10am

I am writing this in the garden of Boughton Court on a glorious morning of bright sunshine but with a gentle breeze quite unlike yesterday's oppressive heat. Grayson had driven Albright into town before I came down for breakfast so I was spared another unpleasant episode.

Alice has a piano lesson and will be busy in the Music Room for at least another hour. Aunt Millicent is meeting with the cook to discuss menus for the upcoming Hunt Ball. I am left alone and am grateful for a little solitude. I've almost finished my books and am trying desperately to come up with an excuse to go into London and find a decent bookstore, preferably alone and avoiding milliners.

Botheration! Just as I'm enjoying the peace and quiet, something comes along to disturb me! It sounds like the servants arguing and it's rude to listen so I guess I'd better move.

11.30am

The morning started well but, like Alice in Wonderland, became curiouser and curiouser. The raised voices came from the small herb patch near the kitchen door and shielded from the landscaped garden by a hedge some six feet in height. I assumed that it was two of the servants who thought the garden to be empty, as they would be unlikely to raise their voices if a member of the family were present. Not wanting to hear the conversation or to have my quiet reading time disrupted, I stood up, hoping they would see me and desist, but the voices continued and got louder. Not wishing them to be embarrassed (and hoping they'd get it over with and go away!) I ducked into the summerhouse but couldn't resist peering through the latticework screen to see what was going on.

Bartram was one of the speakers. Her voice was more shrill than that of the man she was addressing and thus carried further. It seemed that the chap had arranged to meet her on her evening off and accompany her to the pictures, an assignation that he had failed to keep. Bartram also indicated that it had been far too hot for her to be left standing about and that a number of other gentlemen would have been only too eager to view the movie in her company, her wearing her new bonnet and all. (What is it with these English and their hats?).

The male voice had been indistinct at first but as the two of them got closer I was able to discern a hint of a foreign accent, perhaps French, but the voice was too low for me to be sure. Bartram concluded the conversation by announcing that this would be "an end to the matter" and her suitor was summarily dismissed. She stomped back into the house through the kitchen door and he crossed the lawn towards the summer house obviously intending, rather impertinently, to leave through the front gates. He paused to light a cigarette and I got a whiff of strong, sharp Turkish tobacco. The man was too close to my hiding place for my liking so I quietly stepped further back into the summer house, which was partially shuttered and so dark enough to conceal me. It was then that he passed by the window and I realized to my surprise that it was the man I had seen leap from the deck of the New York boat, not drowned after all!

I found it difficult to make small talk over dinner that evening. My mind was spinning with the events of the morning. What was that man doing at Boughton Court? What was his business with Bartram? Had he perhaps traveled to England to be with her? Was he her sweetheart? And, damn it, why wasn't he dead? And now it is bedtime and I still haven't puzzled it out! Mother says that sleeping on a problem often helps so let's see if things are any clearer in the morning.

~ Wednesday 24th June ~

Things were certainly no clearer by breakfast time. Bartram had a face like thunder and I wasn't at all surprised that she broke a plate clearing the table, she clattered the china around so much. Aunt Millicent had wisely decided to breakfast in her room and Uncle and I decided that ignoring the woman was the best option so chatted together about Middle Eastern mythology, a subject in which he was obviously well-versed. He had recently finished a book called *A Summer in Nineveh* which is an account of excavations in ancient Mesopotamia by an archaeologist called Reginald Campbell Thompson, which he thought I might enjoy. I said I would be delighted to borrow it and would collect it from his study after breakfast. That solves my problem of having nothing to read and I am grateful.

Alice was nowhere to be seen. When I inquired of Bartram she said that "Miss Alice has a headache and has gone for a walk. I'll make her some toast later". She said *"toast"* in the tone one might use when referring to a dead snake. Relieved of Alice's company for the second day in succession I rushed to my room and soon became immersed in Thompson's excellent book. I failed to notice the passage of time until my concentration was broken by the lunch gong at 1pm. Alice had not reappeared, much to Aunt Millicent's annoyance. Bartram was dispatched to fetch the girl and reported that Miss Alice's headache was no better and she would take lunch in her room. Aunt Millicent tutted but a tray was prepared and sent up while the rest of us settled to our food.

As the afternoon wore on, still with no sign of my cousin, Aunt Millicent announced that she would investigate and, if Alice were feeling no better, would summon the doctor. She returned to the Morning Room rather more hastily than she'd left and in a considerably more shaky state, repairing immediately to the telephone and requesting that the operator connect her to Inspector Grimes at Guildford Police Station. It appears that Alice's bed had not been slept in, while the French windows onto her balcony were wide open. Alice must have been gone all night.

Aunt Millicent immediately initiated a search of the grounds but nothing was found before the arrival of the police inspector. Grimes spent some time in Alice's room searching for clues then took statements from my Aunt, me and all the staff.

He was interested in the previous day's activity. Had Alice gone off by herself at any point in the afternoon? Had there been any disagreement between her and my Aunt? Except for whether *eau de nil* or mint green was the most stylish choice for a hat, no. I did refer to Aunt Millicent's dizzy spell but that hadn't upset Alice unduly and was quickly resolved by fresh air and smelling salts.

The Inspector made diligent notes, nodded wisely and made his departure without enlightening any of us as to whether he had identified any "leads" on Alice's disappearance. Evening came. My Uncle returned from business and we three sat up together in uneasy silence until midnight, when my Uncle insisted I went to bed.

Recounting the circumstances of my Aunt's fainting fit reminded me of the tiny cut to my hand that I sustained whilst fishing in my bag for the smelling salts. I had intended to find out what had caused the injury and to remove the offending item. Tipping the bag out onto the dressing table I began to pick through the usual paraphernalia. I found my powder compact, a notebook, pen; nothing of note and nothing particularly sharp.

As I went to tidy the things away into the bag, however, I felt something against the lining. I pulled gently and felt it tear away, it was obviously snagged on to the thin silk. It was the figurine, almost forgotten since my arrival in England. I hadn't noticed when I found it that the very tip of the fish tail was broken, showing the base metal; it was needle-sharp. That must have been what had cut my hand.

Raised voices downstairs indicated that Alice had returned. My Aunt alternately scolding and relieved, my Uncle's measured tones. I decided that this was a matter for immediate family only and settled down to sleep.

~ Thursday 25th June ~

When I awoke it was not yet dawn. I was conscious of a presence in the room and as I became more alert I realized that it was making no effort to conceal itself. I turned on the bedside light and saw Alice busily going through my trunk. She had already created quite a pile of items on the floor and was trampling on my favorite scarf. I called out to her to stop, but she paid no attention. I got out of bed and caught her arm. She made no acknowledgment of me, save to shake me off. It appeared that she was in a state of somnambulism.

I decided to rouse my Aunt, but as I moved towards the door Alice dropped the purse she was holding and advanced towards me. Her eyes, which a moment before had been dead and unseeing, suddenly assumed a dangerous glitter. With strength greater than one would suppose in such a slight girl, she grabbed me around the throat with one hand and pushed me against the wall. The voice that emanated from her mouth was quite unlike her normal shrill tones. It was almost masculine, guttural. "Give it to me!"

My throat was so constricted that I could barely answer. "What do you want?" The hand pressed tighter. I could feel my windpipe being crushed and I could no longer speak. Alice released me as I was on the brink of unconsciousness. All I could do was collapse onto the bed. Alice resumed her search.

The noise had woken the household. My Uncle and Aunt appeared, wearing dressing gown. My Uncle was carrying a poker, obviously suspecting an intruder. Alice turned to them, eyes still a-glitter "Give it... to... me!"

Uncle looked bemused. "Give what to you? My dear girl, you are sleepwalking! Let me help you back to bed."

His attempt to take her arm was repulsed with such violence that the elderly gentleman was quite thrown to the ground. Aunt Mildred backed off, terrified, muttering "The girl is possessed!"

The creature that was Alice, the demon in girlish form, approached her mother. "Give it to me!" But all she received in response was a strangled gasp before Aunt Mildred went into one of her swoons.

The Thing-That-Was-Alice's eyes glowed an unearthly red and then she slowly burst into flames.

First a bright blue light appeared around Alice's solar plexus, clearly visible through her nightdress. The light intensified and coalesced into a circle of blue flame resembling a gas ring. As the flames spread Alice returned to her normal self, screaming in her natural voice. At that point Bartram ran in. The noise from my room had obviously been loud enough to reach to the servants' quarters. Alice collapsed when her trunk was no longer able to support the rest of her body. In moments all that remained on the floor were two perfectly preserved legs and the upper portion of the body; the head, chest and arms were untouched. In between was nothing but a pile of silvery ash. The blue flames flickered and died.

It is strange that people's reactions to extreme circumstances can be so varied. Bartram ran to the fireplace and was sick to her stomach. I became quite mechanical in my movements and calmly put on my dressing gown before going downstairs to telephone for Inspector Grimes.

I have tried to recount the night's events in as much detail as possible so that I might not forget anything that might be relevant to the police. The Inspector was woken and is on his way. I have quit the scene, having no wish to stay in the same room as what remains of my cousin. Bartram and I escorted my Uncle and Aunt out to the drawing-room where we are now all waiting for the Inspector to arrive. Seeing that they are both, understandably, in shock I have dispatched Bartram to make tea as I know that is how the English deal with things.

8am

Inspector Grimes has visited the... what? I cannot say it is a crime scene, for there is no evidence of a crime having been committed. All that can be said about the episode is that something jolly peculiar has taken place. It may prove not to be a police matter. Perhaps it was something medical? I am not aware of any condition that would engender spontaneous combustion, however. Grimes summoned the village doctor, more to be seen to be doing something than for any useful purpose. The doctor was, at least, able to sedate Aunt Mildred who had by that point become hysterical, screaming and crying. My Uncle remained quiet, retreating within himself. As Bartram evidently knew of Alice's earlier disappearance but had not informed the family, she was taken off in a police car for further questioning. Eventually Grimes sighed, announced his investigation was concluded and that a file would be prepared for the coroner and made his departure. The doctor telephoned for the undertaker and Alice was scraped up off the floor and removed.

9pm

I have settled on the drawing-room sofa with a blanket. Aunt and Uncle are already asleep after taking the powerful sedative prescribed by their physician. I was offered a dose of the stuff, but declined. The whole day has been utterly dreadful and someone needs to have their wits about them should something else happen.

~ Friday 26th June ~

There is to be a post-mortem examination of Alice's remains today and it is likely she will be buried early next week. Uncle Thomas has gone to his study and my Aunt is staying in bed with nervous exhaustion. The doctor has just left. Only a few days ago I craved solitude but today I would so much rather have Alice's silly chatter and yet another shopping trip! For myself, I am adrift. I really don't know what to do for the best. To stay in my room may give the impression that I am uncaring or disinterested. This could not be further from the truth. Although Alice could be a silly goose, I had felt a genuine liking for my cousin and I do grieve for her. I have written to my mother to advise her of the death of her niece; at least I have spared my Aunt that ordeal. And I have spared my mother the details, simply saying that there had been an accident in the house.

Despite my distress at the death of my cousin I am intrigued by the circumstances of her death. To understand what happened may help me come to terms with it all. The room was fully illuminated and I was certainly awake enough to take the details of the event. Alice was not near the fire ,or any other incendiary sources. She was not carrying a candle; the house has electric light. And there is the matter of the sleepwalking to be considered. I understand that a somnambulist can behave in an extraordinary fashion, given that he is acting out his dream, but Alice's frenzied searching was more focused.

As I think about it, I recall an incident from some years ago. I had gone with a group of friends to a cabaret at a local theater. In between the second-rate comedian and the overblown opera singer came a stage hypnotist who took volunteers from the audience and used the power of mesmerism to convince them to do the most peculiar things for comic effect. One young lady was persuaded that she was swimming the English Channel and waved her arms around enthusiastically, opening and closing her mouth as though taking in and expelling water. A young man squared up for a boxing match with a coat stand, barking his knuckles when he attempted to, as he saw it, punch it in the face. I found the performance slightly embarrassing but there was no doubt that it was well-received by the majority of the audience. I am remembering this now because the glassy-eyed expression on the faces of these stooges, coupled with their complete lack of disregard for their own safety, reminded me of Alice's behavior last night. Could the power of auto suggestion have even caused her self-immolation, I wondered. The human mind is a powerful thing. I must break off my musings as Bartram is here. My Aunt wishes to see me.

1pm

I am writing this in the motor car on the way to Guildford railway station. The interview with my Aunt was not pleasant as we were both very upset. I understand completely her view that under the circumstances it is proper for me to curtail my visit and return home immediately. I am considering my options, however. I have a return passage to New York booked on a liner leaving Southampton in a month and I have a generous allowance. I am not anxious to return to the United States early and should manage perfectly well if I husband my finances, neither do I want to undertake a long journey alone when I am upset. But what to do in a strange country where I don't know anyone?

Grayson has pulled in to the station forecourt. I have resolved to stay the night in the Queen's Hotel there and consider my options. Perhaps I could find more modest accommodation locally and thus eke out my allowance until it is time to return home? It does seem a shame to depart without seeing a little of the mother country. And there is still the mystery of my cousin's death. I am more than a little curious to investigate the phenomenon of her spontaneous combustion and would like to do so while the incident is fresh in my mind. For now I will take the smallest and most basic room in the hotel, a simple supper and bed.

Midnight

It is after midnight and still I cannot sleep! The noise from the next room is incredible. Annoying English upper class braying laughter, the clinking of bottles – how can simply moving a bottle make so much noise? – and a gramophone playing popular dance tunes. It is quite unbearable. I shall complain.

4am

I have finally returned to my bed! Room number 14 turned out to be occupied by Alice's friends Honoria and Bingo who were spending the night in a hotel because Bingo's Crossley Tourer had developed some mechanical fault en route to London. The car had been fixed late that evening and they intended to recommence their journey early the following morning. I didn't point out that is was already early the following morning. They were dancing the Black Bottom when I knocked on the door. Pausing only to wave aside my protestations that it was far too late, that I needed my rest even if they didn't and that I rarely drank alcohol, I soon found myself with a glass of champagne in one hand and winding up the portable gramophone with the other.

It did not take long for the bubbles to take effect and the evening proceeded much in the same vein until the hotel manager advised us that if we persisted in our antics he would be minded to call the constabulary. It is fortunate, perhaps, that ours were the only rooms occupied on that corridor. We finally retired just moments ago. I have promised to meet my friends for breakfast in the morning before they leave for The Smoke (I am getting to grips with the English slang!). I feel suddenly more cheerful; to forget the recent tragic events even temporarily has been a great benefit. Such a shame that they will depart tomorrow.

~ Saturday 27th June ~

I took Honoria aside first thing this morning and told her about Alice. She was, as I expected, very deeply upset. I used a similar form of words to those I had employed when writing to my mother, simply telling Honoria that there had been a fire at Boughton Court and that Alice had been trapped and killed. When she had dried her tears, my new friend inquired as to the cause of the fire. I said I wasn't sure as it had broken out late at night when I was in bed. I did not lie but left her with a very different picture of the night's events than what had actually happened.

When Honoria and Bingo came to leave the poor girl still looked very pale and sad. I'm so sorry I had to give her such bad news, especially as she had been so happy the night before! Bingo gave me a sympathetic look as the porter loaded their luggage into the trunk of the motor. I hugged my friend goodbye and sat in the hotel lounge to consider what to do next. I had a book with me, but couldn't concentrate. I sipped tea, left my biscuits untouched and tried to motivate myself to do something, but it was so difficult. The events of two nights ago repeated themselves, unbidden, in my head like a stuck gramophone record. Suddenly the lounge door opened and there was Honoria. I saw just a flash of her customary mischief, which reassured me that she was already starting to come to terms with the tragedy.

"Neve" she said. "I've just had the most utterly topping idea!"

And I have had an interesting invitation. I could have exchanged my ticket and returned home earlier, but it seemed a pity to make a sea trip all the way to England then start the return journey after only a week. Honoria has suggested I accompany her and Bingo to London. I have no wish to impose, particularly as they lead such busy lives, but a stay in London does sound attractive and I find their company most agreeable. I have proposed a compromise. I will not stay with Honoria and Bingo. After all, our acquaintance is very recent! Instead, I'll take lodgings in the city and we can meet for tea and so on as our schedules permit. This would also give me time to make my long-awaited visit to the British Museum and I can renew my acquaintance with young Archie Glossop! We squeezed both me and my luggage into the back seat of the Crossley and off we went.

~ Sunday 28th June ~

My bags had been hurriedly packed and Bartram was not careful. Clothes were squashed underneath books; dirty and clean garments packed together. I had set about repacking before I checked out of the hotel. As I went through the items I discovered once more the strange little item I had found in my bag. The merman's face wore a baleful expression which was quite justifiable given the poor little thing had had its tail broken off. As I had nothing better to do, I decided that once I reached London I would take it to an antique dealer in the hope of gaining information as to its provenance and an indication of its value. Without giving many details I told Honoria that I had an antique to sell and she recommended a dealer on High Holborn with whom she had dealt in the past and judged to be fair in business.

After seeing my trunk stored securely in the Left Luggage Office at the station I walked into town. The antique dealer was just about to close his store when I arrived but said he was happy to appraise the object given that the pretty American lady had made a special journey. He was young, perhaps only a few years older than myself, and became suddenly animated when I produced the artifact, wrapped carefully in a handkerchief. He screwed a magnifier into one eye, in the manner of a jeweler, and made a careful assay of the thing, confirming that it was indeed Mesopotamian and of some antiquity, perhaps up to a thousand years old. It was indeed made of a base metal plated with an alloy containing a high percentage of gold, and it was worth something in the region of a hundred pounds. Had the lady thought of selling, perhaps?

I said that I was not interested in selling at the moment but I was grateful for the information. The dealer seemed reluctant to give up the piece, however. Was the young miss sure? A hundred pounds would make her stay in London so much more comfortable. His voice assumed a wheedling tone. I eventually lost patience and grabbed the merman back. As I did so I again fell victim to the jagged tail, dripping blood onto the store counter. At that point the young man withdrew, looking angry. Why had I wasted his time when I obviously had no intention of selling the thing? His face reddened in fury, he flung open the door and could not have been more eager to usher me and my tiny artifact out of the store.

How peculiar! His reaction led me to wonder whether the merman was, in fact, worth a great deal more than the amount he had offered.

As my modest means precluded another night at a hotel I decided to spend the remainder of the morning looking for cheaper accommodation. My limited experience of England suggested that store windows were the place to look if one wished to engage staff, buy a second-hand bicycle or seek a bed sitting room. A little store on the corner of New Oxford Street seemed as good a place as any to start with but it proved to be the first of a good many store windows before I found a suitable advertisement. A bed sitting room with shared bathroom and parlor was offered in a house on Grays Inn Road, within easy walking distance of the British Museum but out of the way enough that the rent was reasonable. I called upon the landlady, Mrs Williams, who showed me a simply furnished but neat little room.

The other lodgers were young ladies studying at University College so there would be some intelligent conversation. Breakfast was included in the price and a gas ring in the room would enable me to cook for myself in between times. Mrs Williams was happy for me to take the room for only a month as term was about to end and the other girls would also be vacating the property for the summer. I paid a deposit and now here I am. While the last forty-eight hours have not been wholly pleasant, I have found congenial lodgings, more to my taste than my Aunt's house in many ways. I will be able to further my scholarly interests and I have a delightful new friend. I also popped to the Post Office and telephoned to Honoria in Hampstead to pass on my new address.

10pm

I was tired after staying up until the early hours so decided to retire early. I was tempted to close the window against the traffic noise of the city but it was another stifling evening and I needed fresh air. I heard a fire engine going past, the bell ringing then fading into the distance. An emergency was obviously being dealt with.

I turned down the oil lamp and was about to settle into sleep when there was a sharp sound at the window. It came again then a few bits of gravel sailed through the opening and landed on the night stand. Feeling more than a little apprehensive, I kept the light off and edged the curtain back a little. Bingo's smart black motor was parked directly below the window and leaning against it was my new best friend Honoria. A stylishly dressed chap looked up and waved. It was Archie! How lovely! I waved back, threw on my dressing-gown and crept downstairs. The other residents were obviously in bed as the house was in darkness.

Honoria embraced me enthusiastically. "Darling, I know we weren't going to meet until Friday but we are all off to an utterly divine supper club in Soho. We can't leave you alone on your first night in London!" She gave me a look of mock pleading. "Oh do say you'll come along! We'd simply love you to meet our friends." Perhaps it wasn't so late after all. And it was probably best to go with them before they woke my new neighbors. I dressed quickly, hoping my clothes would pass muster on the London jazz scene, then hopped into the back of the motor. Bingo revved the engine and tore off towards the West End. The Cosmopolitan was not quite as divine as Honoria had painted it, being a dingy basement with a bar and indifferent catering but the company was excellent and the champagne flowed. I was surprised at how delighted I felt that Archie was there too. Conversation was difficult over the sound of the band but when they took a break Archie and I had an opportunity to talk. He expressed his sorrow at hearing of Alice's death before we went on to talk of happier things.

A research paper Archie had written summarizing his preliminary findings on the Mesopotamian treasures had recently been accepted for publication in a very prestigious journal; he was very excited about that. Being by that time rather tipsy, I confided that I had a teensy Mesopotamian artifact right there in my purse. He said he'd like to take a look and I said to be careful as it was very, very valuable. Archie had a peek, agreed and asked me to take it in to the museum the following day as he'd like to look at it more closely. The band started up again and Honoria dragged me onto the dance floor. We danced until the place closed and Bingo, somewhat the worse for drink, dropped me back at my lodgings.

~ Monday 29th June ~

I met the other residents at breakfast. I was relieved that no-one commented on my nocturnal comings and goings; either I had been quiet enough or they were demonstrating typical English middle class politeness. There are three other girls, students called Louise, Joan and Mary who seem like agreeable sorts. We exchanged some polite conversation before our landlady provided a welcome interruption by delivering another pot of tea and yet more toast. As she set the comestibles down on the table she inquired if anyone had heard the fire engine last night. We all had, and she was obviously thrilled to disclose that the fire engine had been on its way to an incident in High Holborn.

She believed it was a fire in an antique store. According to her friend the Post Mistress, whose husband was one of the attending firemen, the fire had been a peculiar one. The store itself was hardly damaged but the antique dealer himself had been severely burned and died in the infirmary shortly afterwards.

A fire in the same street as the store of the dealer I had visited yesterday and, by the sounds of it, a death in similar circumstances to Alice's. For my own sanity I had to reassure myself that the fire had not been in the same store. Directly after breakfast I walked back to the store to investigate the incident for myself.

I found no reassurance there. The dealer's store did not look as if it had suffered a fire. There was no evidence of scorching or smoke on the outside of the building but a black curtain had been hung across the window to prevent anyone seeing in. The building had been cordoned off and a policeman stood outside, presumably to preserve evidence and also because some of the antiquities therein were of considerable monetary value. I didn't feel able to interview the constable; it would have been odd for a complete stranger (and a foreigner) to be so curious about the details of the fire. I certainly had no wish to implicate myself in the matter, given that I had been in the store the previous day and could well have left my fingerprints lying about. Instead I took a walk and tried to marshal my thoughts about what had happened.

It appeared that two very similar incidents had occurred in quick succession. My cousin Alice had been partially incinerated before my eyes and the antique dealer had apparently expired in a similar fashion within twenty four hours of her death. Do cases of this nature come in clusters, perhaps? Could the geography of the area be to blame? Is South East England on some kind of geological fault, leaking gas that then ignites? If so, why are only people and not property damaged? So many questions! If I am to investigate this mystery I first of all need to find out more about the phenomenon. London is blessed with a great many book stores and I did not need to walk far before I found a large one that obviously catered to the many students in the area. I was again concerned about appearing odd, as I am sure young women rarely seek to purchase books on such matters.

Rather than inquiring with an assistant, therefore, I started by browsing the science section, but neither volumes on chemistry or biology yielded any useful clues. After some minutes a store girl came over and asked if she could help me. Admitting that my query may sound rather peculiar I told her what I was looking for. She wondered if I had read any Charles Dickens. When I shook my head she led me to the fiction shelves and selected *Bleak House*.

"This may help with your question, miss," she smiled. "That'll be one and ninepence, please!"

As the British Museum was between the book store and my new lodgings I decided to make that call upon Archie. His office was tucked away in a corner on the third floor of the building up a somewhat rickety staircase. It was small, dusty and full of interesting things on shelves. Books and journals occupied most of the space and all of them had bits of paper sticking out marking sections of interest and often with notes written on them.

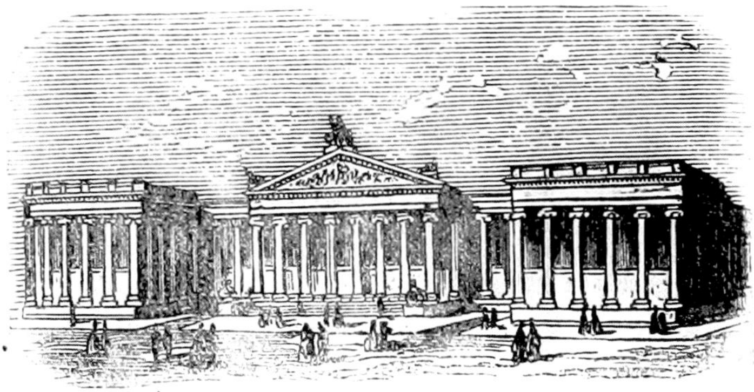

Some very old pottery took up the top shelf of the bookcase, one item of which caused Archie to blush – he seems to do that with very little provocation – it's so charming! – as he whisked it into his desk drawer.

Archie was able to examine my little merman much more successfully in daylight. He pronounced it to be around three thousand years old; the dealer had either lied or been mistaken, but he did confirm the dealer's hypothesis that it was Sumerian. Archie did not attempt to place a monetary value on the thing, but said that it would be of considerable value to his research. I immediately offered to loan the merman to him, instinct telling me that he would take the utmost care of it.

He thanked me and offered me a cup of tea in return. He scrabbled around in the desk, eventually finding a packet of slightly soft ginger nut biscuits and we chatted companionably about his research. He had to attend a meeting with a professor later that morning so our tea was over too soon but we arranged to meet for supper the following evening.

I took a walk after leaving the museum, returning to my room in the afternoon. I opened the brown paper parcel from the book store and flicked through the pages of *Bleak House.* I had tried to read Dickens a few years earlier but found him overly sentimental and not always believable. I was unwilling to cause offense in a country that holds the man in great reverence so thought it discreet to simply plead ignorance of his work to the store assistant despite the fact that Dickens is very popular in the United States too.

I was not drawn into the story on this occasion either. Bleak House is a convoluted tale of an unresolved court case and did not appear at first glance to offer any hope of a resolution to either the dramatis personae or my problem. The second time around I spent slightly longer skimming each individual page and found this in Chapter 32, wherein is discovered the death of the gin-sodden Mr Krook:

> *"Mr. Guppy takes the light. They go down, more dead than alive, and holding one another, push open the door of the back store. The cat has retreated close to it and stands snarling, not at them, at something on the ground before the fire. There is a very little fire left in the grate, but there is a smouldering, suffocating vapour in the room and a dark, greasy coating on the walls and ceiling. The chairs and table, and the bottle so rarely absent from the table, all stand as usual. On one chair-back hang the old man's hairy cap and coat."*
>
> and
>
> *"Here is a small burnt patch of flooring; here is the tinder from a little bundle of burnt paper, but not so light as usual, seeming to be steeped in something; and here is—is it the cinder of a small charred and broken log of wood sprinkled with white ashes, or is it coal? Oh, horror, he IS here! And this from which we run away, striking out the light and overturning one another into the street, is all that represents him...*
>
> *Call the death by any name your Highness will, attribute it to whom you will, or say it might have been prevented how you will, it is the same death eternally—inborn, inbred, engendered in the corrupted humours of the vicious body itself, and that only—spontaneous combustion, and none other of all the deaths that can be died."*

Although Dickens did not detail the event as it happened but rather the aftermath, there were significant similarities between the fictional account and the real incident. Alice, thank heavens, did not leave any great amount of greasy residue behind. I am grateful for that as to have overseen the clearing-up would have considerably distressed my Aunt and the process would have been unpleasant and irksome for the servants. Alice's middle section was the only part of her body destroyed, whereas Krook was completely reduced to ashes. I noted that Krook died alone, which was also true of the man in the antique store. Comparing Dickens' account with what I witnessed at Boughton Court and the little information I had about the death in the store, I saw a great deal of commonalities. I have no idea what conclusions the Surrey Constabulary had drawn about the death of my cousin but I have reached the certainty that Alice was a victim of spontaneous human combustion. How, though? And why? And why had this also happened to the oleaginous antiques seller?

My musings were interrupted by a knock on the door. Joan's merry face peeped round and summoned me to the parlor. Her grandmother had sent her a large and delicious-looking fruit cake and Mrs Williams had put the kettle on. I was distracted for a couple of hours by cheery conversation and excellent food. Although my stay in England has been short, I have learned that there is very little which cannot be put right by a pot of tea and I did not demur when Mary set to with a toasting fork and produced a good plate of hot crumpets. Time was getting on and my jolly companions had work to prepare for the following day so withdrew to their rooms. I had no wish to be on my own with my thoughts so I offered to help Mrs Williams wash the tea things; an offer which she was happy to accept.

Although my staying there was a business arrangement the house was a friendly one and helping out with a little drying up and putting away was more an excuse to continue our conversation than it was an inappropriate blurring of the role of landlady and tenant.

As we worked, Mrs Williams passed on the local gossip (there seemed to be little the woman didn't know; she was better than the wireless!) and the conversation turned eventually to the fire of the previous evening.

No further details had been forthcoming from the relative of the fireman but Mrs Williams' niece Margery was walking out with a young man who had been to school with the deceased gentleman so my landlady was aware that the funeral would be in two day's time, at St George's Church. At that point I realized with horror that I did not have the details of Alice's funeral, nor had I established whether my Aunt considered it appropriate for me to attend. I curtailed our chat and hurried to the Post Office to send a telegram both requesting information on the arrangements for Alice's final journey and appraising my Aunt of my whereabouts.

After returning from the Post Office I went to my room and heated some canned soup on the gas ring which, with bread, formed a simple supper. I sat at the desk with a large piece of paper and cataloged the mysteries so far:

1. The disappearance and later spontaneous combustion of my cousin Alice and the subsequent incident in the antiques store.

2. The apparent death and resurrection of the man on the liner, and how he'd happened to fetch up in a country garden in Surrey.

3. The valuable golden merman.

I felt unable to progress any further on the matter of the deaths. I had proceeded rationally thus far, but Alice's demise had shaken me and I feared some form of delayed shock might affect me in the days to come. I turned, therefore, to Bartram's foreign suitor. This was the first time I had been able to fully collect my thoughts for some days and once I set my full attention to the problem I concluded quickly that The Drowned Man had cultivated Bartram's attentions to gain access to my Aunt's household.

It also occurred to me that he might have had a hand in Alice's disappearance which had led, either directly or indirectly to her death. And moments before she died Alice had been in my room looking for something. This must have been the tiny merman.

All right then. So The Drowned Man had stowed away on the ship with the merman before accidentally dropping it as he leapt over the side, faking his death to throw the ship's officer off his trail. Quite how he was able to survive in the water I have no idea.

Once we'd landed at London he'd taken steps to find me and recover the statuette. Maybe he'd been able to trace the registration plates on the Bentley. He'd befriended Bartram in order to get into the house but she, being such a sour puss, had rejected him quick-smart when he stood her up at the picture palace, leading to the quarrel I'd overheard in the garden and him stomping off through the front gate. So far the hypothesis hung together well but didn't altogether explain later events.

The Drowned Man may have engineered Alice's disappearance – she seemed the type who'd easily be charmed away – but her actions after her return and the circumstances of her death still make no sense. When The Drowned Man visited Boughton Court why did he leave by the front gate? The likelihood of someone seeing an intruder was extremely high and my Aunt would have been on the telephone to the police like a shot. Come to think of it, why didn't I raise the alarm?

So many thoughts all pouring out onto the paper!

I heard the grandfather clock in the downstairs hall strike midnight and decided to end my investigations for the night. I had made some headway at least and would formulate a plan for further inquiry in the morning.

~ Tuesday 30th June ~

I write this after a night of very little sleep. So many unanswered questions made it difficult to settle. Once I had fallen asleep my dreams took me back to the night Alice died in my room and I lived again the blue flames that took my cousin away before I woke covered in sweat and terrified. I tossed and turned and tried to get back to sleep but something else had begun nagging at me. Turning over in my mind the events of the last day at Boughton Court I realised that one more thing didn't make sense.

Bartram had been into Alice's room at least twice between when she disappeared and when my Aunt realized she'd gone. She'd reported to Aunt Millicent that Alice was unwell and would prefer to take her meals in her room, but my Aunt had later discovered that Alice's bed had not been slept in. It appears that Bartram was complicit in Alice's disappearance, which I was beginning to view as an abduction. I wondered if the police inspector had made that connection when he interviewed Bartram and that was why she had been taken away for questioning. By then the room was bright with early morning sunlight despite the drapes so I gave up trying to get back to sleep and recorded my thoughts in this diary.

It was not long before the household was up and about. Joan and Mary were already tucking into scrambled eggs and a large quantity of toast when I went downstairs but Louise was not yet at the table, which Mary said was peculiar as she tended towards early rising. I offered to rouse her and went back upstairs to her room, which was at the back of the house down a short passage and slightly out of the way of the other bedrooms. I tapped on the door, which was slightly ajar. As there was no answer I hoped Louise would not think it impolite for me to go in and wake her rather more directly. She thanked me for the call, blamed a faulty alarm clock and hurried off to wash.

As I descended again I heard a bump behind me. I knew that all the other occupants of the house apart from Louise were in the kitchen. I retraced my steps again and heard shuffling sounds from my own room, followed by another bump. Intrigued, I opened the door. Suddenly a strange smell assailed me.

1pm

I've never felt less like writing. I have the worst headache and it's so dark in here that I can hardly see to put the words on the page. It is vital that I make a record, though, as it may eventually provide evidence in a court of law. I hope that the case will be the trial of my abductors, not of my murderers.

The strange smell must have been chloroform; my watch tells me that several hours have passed since I went into my room and I am certainly no longer at Mrs Williams' house. I am now in a wooden crate. There is a little light coming through gaps between the planks and my captors have not felt the need to tie me up, the lid of the crate being firmly nailed shut. I am grateful for being able to move a little but I am still suffering from the most dreadful cramp and would very much like to stretch out my legs.

I have been placed in a sitting position with my head close to the roof of the crate, which must be about three feet square. My captors have left my bag with me, although I can tell they've gone through it. I'm guessing they were looking for the merman which is, thankfully, with Archie Glossop. I wish I'd gotten rid of the damn thing earlier!

Midnight

A loud noise roused me from my soporific state. This was swiftly followed by a tremendous jolting. I was grateful that I had not eaten that day as the combination of the anesthetic and the motion made me feel extremely sick. I realized that I must be in some kind of vehicle and as I focused more on the sound it appeared that I was on a train, probably in the guard's van. After several stops and some hours I felt the crate being unloaded. I banged and shouted but whoever was handling this piece of priceless US cargo must have been in cahoots with my captors as the response was the heavy thud of a fist on the side of the crate and someone telling me to shut up.

I have no idea where I am, but it's not in London.

~ Wednesday 1st July ~

It is morning and I am in the countryside somewhere. The journey went on for hours, so I'm guessing we must be far from London. I couldn't see much once the train had stopped. It was dark out, so no light penetrated the gaps between the planks of the crate. There was a lot more bumping and I got pretty shaken up as my prison was loaded onto a cart – there was a distinct smell of horse – and the journey from the station wasn't smooth like a road but more like a dirt track. I've never been outside of London before but I guess we must be somewhere far from any city as this place was real quiet apart from me hollering to be let out.

Eventually the cart stopped and the lid was levered up. I could barely stand after being squashed up for so long and they took advantage of this to clap a cloth soaked in more chloroform over my mouth and nose. I woke up this morning lying on a bed in an old cottage. The window to my room has been nailed shut, but I can see a little garden outside and a beach beyond that.

A man came to get me. From his accent I could tell that he was the one who'd told me to be quiet the night before. He didn't say much but I think he's Scottish. Perhaps we're in Scotland then? He was a lot taller and bigger than me and very strong. I tried to fight back but he grabbed both my wrists and held them before half dragging, half carrying me downstairs.

Part of me wasn't surprised to see The Drowned Man there. He was sitting at a table with a teapot and sandwiches in front of him. It all looked very civilized but I was in no mood for a tea party.

"What in the name of all that's holy is this?" I yelled, more angry than frightened.

Imagine a lizard smiling. He looked like that.

"There is very little here that is holy, Miss Selcibuc. Are you a religious woman, I wonder? Will your God come to your rescue, do you think?"He waved to a chair beside his own. "Sit. Have some tea."

"I don't think so!" I spat back. "Let me out of here now before I scream the goddamn place down."

"Please feel free". The reptilian smirk again. "I should enjoy that. We're about thirty miles from the nearest town so you can shriek your little heart out. In fact you should, then I won't have to rip it out myself."

"If you're trying to scare me, I'll say that you've got the wrong gal!" I snapped back.

"You're a challenge. I like that."

He grabbed my arm suddenly and in one swift movement bent it back behind me. The pain was excruciating. I jumped up and kicked the chair over but he didn't let go. He called for the goon who'd fetched me downstairs and between the two of them they got my hands and feet tied to the chair. It was pointless to try and get free, at least while they were watching me. I made up my mind to save my strength until I had a realistic chance of escape. Soon it was just me and The Drowned Man.

"Now Miss Selcibuc, I think you have something that belongs to me. It's very precious, a family heirloom you might say. Why not just hand it over and we'll say no more about it?" He leaned in close to me and I felt the cold steel of a knife gently stroke against my throat.

"I don't have anything" I gasped. "You want the little statue? It's in London. I don't have it. It's safe and you won't get it."

"The statue, yes. Yes, that's part of it. I want the little statue. But I need something else as well."

The Drowned Man put down the knife and produced a cigarette lighter from the pocket of his jacket. He took a candle from the mantelshelf.

"You see this candle, Miss Selcibuc? Without the flame it gives no light. So I apply the lighter, so, and here is the light. So it is with the merman. On its own, no light. With the lovely Miss Selcibuc there is much light!" This seemed to amuse him and he chuckled to himself for a moment before grabbing the candle and thrusting it into my face. "The candle is very pretty, yes? It makes a pleasing light but it can also destroy. Oh yes, it is very destructive."

He was so close that the smell of rotten fish almost overwhelmed me. It was then that I noticed something strange about him – he had slits behind his ears. They didn't seem to be from an injury – they were open cuts but healthily pink, not scars or wounds. He brushed the candle flame lightly against my cheek and I could feel it burn. I gritted my teeth.

"You monster!"

"Miss Selcibuc! Is that any way for a well-brought up young lady to talk?"

His face was close enough for me to send some well-aimed spittle his way. Then he hit me. Hard.

"Go back to your room, Miss Selcibuc. We'll talk again later. And don't waste energy trying to escape."

Once I was back in the bedroom my fear abated somewhat and I was able to think about what he'd said. Something about applying the lighter to the candle. Then I had a thought which should have occurred to me much earlier. Both Alice and the antiques dealer had been not just in my company but in the company of the merman shortly before they died and on both occasions I had cut myself.

Was it possible that my blood had somehow triggered the weird blue flames that had led to their deaths?

Stunned, I contemplated my involvement, albeit unintentional, in the deaths of two innocent people. That was nonsense, of course, I told myself. The merman was just a pretty trinket, me cutting myself a coincidence. I did think, however, that if I'd had the thing with me at that moment I would have had another go to see if the magic worked on The Drowned Man. I wouldn't have minded seeing him burn horribly.

Magic? In the absence of a more rational explanation it would do as a working hypothesis. So let's think this through. The merman has some kind of magical ability that is activated by human blood. Once it is active it sets things on fire. No, it sets *people* on fire. Specifically, it sets people that try to take it from me on fire. Alice had been looking for it in my bag, the dealer was most anxious that I sell it to him, but it didn't affect me when I'd appropriated it from the Drowned Man, although he wanted it back enough to pursue me from Southampton and kidnap me to heaven knows where.

And if it was magical and I was the key, exactly how much of my blood did The Drowned Man need in order to activate it? I fought to pull myself together. If my theory was correct, The Drowned Man wouldn't hurt me too much until me and the merman were in the same place. He'd want to conserve my blood for whatever he had planned. I shuddered to think about that.

My family on my Daddy's side were of good pioneer stock. I was damned if my family line would die now. I mentally pulled my wagons into a circle and looked for a means of escape, struggling to take a hold of my whirling thoughts and to focus. It seemed to me that using the merman as a bargaining tool would give me the best chance. My bedroom door was, of course, locked. I hammered on it and yelled.

"OK, you win! I'll tell you where to get the merman!"

After a few minutes I heard footsteps on the stairs. They were light, so probably The Drowned Man rather than his Scottish sidekick. Yes, it was The Drowned Man.

"I thought you could be persuaded to see sense." That lizard smile again. A fly buzzed against the window and I imagined his tongue flicking out to devour it.

"The merman is in London with a friend of mine, Lavinia Thompson," I lied. "If I can telephone to Lavinia she can arrange to send it to me. But you must promise, please, on your honor as a gentleman that you will release me once you have it". If the truth be told I thought it unlikely that he possessed any honor and he obviously was no gentleman but my ploy coupled with his evident greed for the artifact did the trick.

"Very well. McDonald will drive us to the Post Office and you can telephone this Thompson woman from there. I will be with you all the time and if you try any nonsense..." He drew his finger across his throat, making a hissing noise.

If my theory about how the merman worked was correct, he was bluffing just as much as I was. My blood had proved suited to activating the thing and I guessed and conjectured that not everyone was able to do that. If my guess was accurate, it was in his interests to keep me alive at least until he had the merman.

A small van was parked outside the cottage, to my relief. I found the idea of a thirty mile journey by horse and cart decidedly unappealing. The drive was unpleasant enough, much of it being on dirt tracks before we eventually joined a properly metaled road and, in due course, another major road. There were few signposts but I did see one that said Aberdeen 15 Miles. The Drowned Man noted what I had seen and ordered McDonald to pull over while he blindfolded me. I could see from the position of the sun that we were heading west.

Before we reached Aberdeen, however, the van halted and The Drowned Man uncovered my eyes. We were outside a small village post office where there would be a telephone. Thankfully I had memorized Honoria's number. Fortune had further favored me by putting the telephone in a corner at such an angle that The Drowned Man wasn't able to get in close. I asked for Hampstead 7934 as quietly as possible and hoped he hadn't overheard. A few moments later I heard a cheery "Hallo, hallo! Hampstead 7934". Bingo, thank heavens!

"Hello, Lavinia this is Neve. I'm sorry I couldn't meet you for lunch yesterday but I wondered if you'd mind sending me something?"

Bingo was a bit of a rum cove, but he was no-one's fool. "Neve, are you all right?"

"I'm having a lovely time, darling. I'm on holiday. Could you please send the little blue box I left at your house to the Post Office at..." I checked the information on the telephone dial "Balmedie? It's a rather spiffy brooch. Got a very important party to go to!"

"Righty-ho old chum. Toodle pip!" And Bingo rang off.

I don't know how much Bingo had got from that conversation but he'd seemed to get the idea that something was wrong. Now I just had to wait it out and hope that he worked out that there was no little blue box and that I was somewhere near Balmedie.

~ 2nd-4th July ~

The last two days would have been extremely dull had the tedium not been interspersed with moments of blind panic. It was late afternoon by the time we got back to the cottage and McDonald immediately dragged me up the stairs to my room and locked me in. It was clear that nothing more was to be done until "Lavinia" sent the merman. I dreaded to think what would happen if The Drowned Man did somehow get hold of the thing.

A couple of hours later McDonald came up with a tray of sandwiches and a tin mug of water. There was nothing hot in case I threw it in his face and ran for it. The only sanitary facilities in the room were a jug of cold water and a bowl for washing and a chamber pot. I had the indignity of watching McDonald leave with my waste in a pot. Horrible!

And that was it until Monday evening. I lay on the bed and watched the sun sink slowly below the horizon, but I couldn't sleep. My host had not been thoughtful enough to provide a nightgown and I didn't want to risk either of the creeps seeing me in a state of undress. All I had with me was my bag with a little money, my diary and the usual feminine accoutrements; my hairbrush, compact, a handkerchief. My wristwatch enabled me to keep track of the time. I missed the chiming grandfather clock at Gray's Inn Road.

Dawn comes early in Scotland in summer. I lay on the bed as the room slowly lightened. Suddenly I heard the sound of a car horn outside. Bingo's Crossley! I threw the drapes open and sure enough there were Bingo and Archie waving up at me just as if we were off for a night on the town.

"Hurry up, old thing!" Archie called and then, in an appallingly bad American accent, "Time to split this hyer joint!" The situation might have been dire but I laughed despite myself. The chaps had not arrived quietly and my captors were unlikely to give them a ticker tape welcome.

I heard a shot ring out and ding off the Crossley's wing mirror.

"I say! Take care, old man. This is premium British engineering" shouted Bingo. Another shot, then I saw McDonald emerge through the front door. This was obviously the scenario Bingo and Archie had planned for. The final shot came from Bingo's revolver (Bingo had a revolver?) and the goon fell to the ground. My two friends charged through the door and I heard the sound of feet hurrying down the stairs. Then The Drowned Man was yelling in the hallway. He was not speaking English but I could tell from the tone that he was employing every cuss word at his disposal.

There was much scuffling and banging about then a heavy, dull thud. I heard Bingo yell out but I couldn't work out what he'd said. Feet thundered up the stairs and I heard Archie on the other side of the bedroom door.

"Neve, get away from the door. Shout when you're clear."

"I'm standing on the bed. I'm clear!"

Archie threw his whole weight against the door which shook and shuddered. A few seconds later he did it again and once more before the lock splintered and he half-fell into my room.

"Darling, are you all right?" he gasped. "Let's get you out of here before that bally scoundrel wakes up".

I hadn't realized how badly my ordeal had affected me until I tried to move. As I stepped down off the bed my legs wobbled and gave way and I collapsed back on to it. Archie came over to help and I'm ashamed to say I started sobbing. He put a protective arm around me and helped me, slowly, to descend the stairs.

Bingo hadn't been idle while Archie was rescuing me. The Drowned Man had been trussed up like a Thanksgiving turkey and dumped unceremoniously outside the front door. Bingo and Archie helped me into the back of the motor and fussed around no end, making sure that I had enough rugs and offering me sips of brandy from a hip flask. Then Archie's face grew serious. "Close your eyes, Neve". I didn't want to, but I complied. There was another shot and then Bingo revved the engine and the Crossley pulled away.

"Cheerio, you cad! Good riddance to bad rubbish!"

I was shivering despite the warm weather. Archie said it was shock and that the brandy would help but they were going to drive to the nearest town and get me looked at by a doctor before we returned to London. Under the circumstances he suggested that we probably shouldn't call the police.

I was intrigued about how they'd found me.

"Oh that's easy, old thing" said Bingo. "I was at Cambridge with one of the local laird's sons. His pater owns half of Aberdeenshire, including the village you telephoned from. I had a little chat to Mervyn on the old dog and bone and got him to poke about a bit. He had a squizz at the letting records from his father's estate and found out that that one of the estate cottages had been rented just a day or two ago by a chappie who paid a month's rent up front in cash. Put two and two together and reckoned it was worth a punt. And young Archie here rather fancied a run out." So the information I had given them about the location of the Post Office had been useful insofar as it confirmed my general location. There was a substantial town within ten miles of my prison; The Drowned Man and McDonald must have driven around some to confuse me. We broke our journey there and I saw the town doctor at Archie's insistence. We told him that I'd been feeling faint and hadn't been eating. His verdict was that there was nothing wrong a decent lunch wouldn't put right but what I really yearned for was a hot bath.

The run back to London would take a couple of days anyway, and once we'd satisfied Archie's anxiety about my health and welfare I was keen to get as far away from that darned cottage as possible. Bingo declared that he loved the open road and the wind in his hair, pulled on his driving goggles and pulled down a loud check cap and off we went rather faster than was sensible. Bingo might have been a tad reckless but the roads were clear and we made it over the border into England before nightfall. We took lodgings in a pretty country inn. Bingo and Archie shared the room next to mine as I didn't want to be too far away from my friends. I couldn't escape the fear that The Drowned Man would find me somehow. For now there was a hot meal, a hot bath and a warm, comfortable bed. Heaven!

All my dreams were nightmares that night. I woke screaming in the small hours and Archie came to comfort me. "Archie," I said, "Bingo shot that man, didn't he?" Archie didn't say anything. He just and nodded. "How could Bingo do that to another human being?" I gasped.

"Neve, that creature was not a human being. Every day he lived you were in terrible danger. Go to sleep now." I fought sleep but my eyes closed anyway. The hotel landlady woke me with a tray of tea. It was mid-morning and my conversation with Archie seemed like just another nightmare.

~ Sunday 5th July ~

We motored in a more leisurely fashion today and easily reached London by late afternoon. Bingo drove directly to the house in Hampstead where Honoria was waiting anxiously.

"Neve! Oh thank God you're all right. We were so worried. First Alice and then..." she broke off with tears in her eyes. "Not to worry old thing. All serene now!" laughed Archie, jollying her along. She smiled and hurried off to put the kettle on.

Honoria wouldn't hear of me returning to Mrs Williams'. She said it was far more of an imposition to be worrying about my safety all day and night than it would be for her to have me staying.

Honoria was clearly in no mood to argue so I assented. It was agreed that Bingo and I would drive over to Grays Inn Road the following day to collect my belongings and I would take possession of a small attic bedroom, close enough for Honoria to keep an eye on me, but quiet enough for me to have a little privacy if required.

~ Monday 6th July ~

Honoria insisted that I should rest following the Scottish episode, but I felt quite well this morning and after a late breakfast I decided to visit Archie at work. This was to be my first experience of London's omnibuses, but I managed to navigate with reasonable ease the route to Archie's office and arrived in time to whisk him off to Lyons Corner House for lunch.

After the Nippy had brought our ham salad and a pot of strong tea Archie and I settled to a discussion on the merman. I shared my suspicions about a link between the merman and the deaths of Alice and the antiques dealer, feeling like a prize idiot for even suggesting that magic was involved.

Archie had already assured himself of its antiquity and said that further study carried out after I'd passed the thing into his care had led him to categorize it as a votive object; that is, an object designed for veneration. It is likely that the merman was originally crafted for use on a household altar. Further, he believed it to be one of a number of objects discovered in Nineveh and that had subsequently been reported missing presumed stolen. As if that wasn't enough, what Archie said next rather took me aback. He felt he had gone as far as he could in analyzing the merman and the next step would be to consult an expert in the esoteric use of such objects.

Did Archie believe that the merman did indeed have magical powers? It seemed to me extraordinary that a well-educated chap such as my friend would believe in such things but then again, the possibility had entered my own head and I do not consider myself to be superstitious or gullible. I assented and asked if I could go with him when he took the merman to be appraised. Archie agreed but cautioned me that the expert was not in the academy, as he put it, but was none other than the odious Mr Albright. I hadn't realized that the two men knew each other. There had been no hint of any kind of relationship at Aunt Millicent's dinner party. The only time that had spoken to each other that evening was when Albright's behavior crossed the line of acceptability and Archie felt honor-bound to step in.

"Albright's a rum cove," Archie explained. "I try and avoid the man as much as possible but he is a valuable source of rare books and the occasional old item. Heaven knows where he gets them from. I think it best not to inquire into his sources. Anyway, if you need to know about the use of votive objects in the magic of ancient civilizations then Albright's your man.

"Neve, if we are going to investigate fully what this thing is capable of – and there is the possibility that it's not capable of anything magical at all – you will need to be there. You said that the fires happened after your blood got onto the merman. Nothing happened when it was simply in your possession. Also, what The Drowned Man said to you suggests that you were in some way able to activate the thing unconsciously."

I saw the turn that the conversation was taking. Archie wanted to try my blood on the merman to see what would happen. I was worried.

"Archie, Alice didn't even touch the merman and she died. What if we call up something and it burns us." Truth be told, I was less concerned about any ill-effects befalling Albright.

"That's why we need our Ebenezer. He'll probably have some millennia-old scroll or another that'll cast some light on the matter and if there are any references to this kind of magic in the ancient texts, they should tell us how it works and how to control it. I'm not aware of anything in either the British Museum or the Institute of Archaeology's collections, so unfortunately we need to pay a visit to one of the most revolting men ever to draw breath." He smiled. "Sorry about that, old top. Ready to go?"

It was a short walk from Tottenham Court Road to Museum Street. Albright's store was small and dingy. The window display was not immediately appealing, consisting of a number of small terracotta pots and lamps on cheap wooden shelving. Through the window I could see shelves of books in the dimly-lit interior. I noticed that Archie took a deep breath before pushing open the door.

The store door was fitted with a bell that didn't so much ring as rattle, but was loud enough to summon Albright through a door that led, I thought, to a store room or perhaps a kitchen. The musty smell of books that clung to him habitually permeated the room. There was no store counter or till, but a small schoolroom desk occupied one corner of the store. On it was a receipt book and on the floor beside it were large rolls of brown paper and string.

The rest of the store was similarly cluttered. Books lay in piles at intervals on the floor while the center of the store was occupied by a large rug which had at one time been pale green, I think, but was now an unattractive shade of khaki.

Albright seemed surprised to see us. The thick layer of dust covering every surface suggested that he didn't get too many customers. There was no welcoming smile, nor did I expect one. He shuffled over to Archie, getting very close before he muttered "Glossop. What do you want?"

Archie explained that we were looking for Albright's opinion on a small artifact which had recently come into the collection of the British Museum. This white lie was, I know, told to protect me and I was grateful.

The merman had been carefully wrapped in layers of felt before being placed in a small wooden box. Archie handed the entire package over to Albright who took it over to the desk and began to unwrap it. He took great care over this process, producing a velvet covered pad from a drawer and placing the merman on it. Hc took a magnifying glass from the same drawer together and spent some minutes scrutinizing the object, turning it gently. Finally, and oddly, he sniffed it and touched it, just for a second, with the tip of his tongue.

"It's been used fairly recently. In the last two weeks, I'd say". I had imagined that Albright would begin his appraisal in the same way as Archie and the dealer had: age, provenance, cash value. But Albright was as unorthodox in this as he was in his table manners. His inspection complete he moved quickly to the door of the store, turned the sign to Closed and locked it firmly. Then he turned to me.

"Miss Selcibuc, perhaps you and Mr Glossop would step this way?" He indicated the door to the back room whence he had come some minutes earlier. I hesitated. Archie, his normally cheerful face very grave, nodded assent and we entered the back room. Albright followed us in and closed the door but did not lock it, which was a relief to me.

The room was lined with bookshelves, like the store, but there was no other furniture. The floor was almost totally covered with a worn Chinese carpet. It had obviously fallen foul of more than one moth infestation and was peppered with burn marks which I guessed were either from a candle or one of Albright's cigarettes.

Ushering us to one side, Albright swiftly rolled up the carpet. The floor underneath was of bare floorboards that had been sanded and varnished but so long ago that the varnish had turned very dark and was considerably scraped and scratched. What was truly remarkable, though, was that in the center of the floor was a full magic circle. I knew enough about the things to identify that that was what it was but anyone who'd ever read a fairytale, even, would be able to work that out. The circle was made up of a number of concentric bands all picked out in red or white paint. The outer circle was in Latin, which was perhaps to be expected, but none of the glyphs beyond that corresponded with any language I had ever seen. Not Latin, not Greek or Cyrillic either. In the center of the circle was a pentagram, that universal symbol of diabolism. Overlaid on that design was a creature very similar in shape to the merman but about two feet across. Albright put the merman, still on its little green cushion, onto the pentagram-and-merman design before stepping back out of the circle, bowing reverently.

"This is weird," I whispered to Archie, who motioned me to be quiet.

Albright took a bundle from one of the shelves. Unfolded, it was a dark blue robe. He took off his jacket and put it on, knotting a light blue cord around his waist. He closed the curtains and lit an oil lamp that was on the floor in one corner. Then he raised his arms and began to chant.

"Ia! Ia! Ia Dagon. Ia! Ia! Ia Hydra! Hail to the father and mother of the waters whence comes all life. Attend us now in our solemn rite!"

The shadows cast by the light seemed to change and to move. No, they were definitely moving, there was no illusion. The shadows spun faster and faster and it felt like I was watching some huge, crazy zoetrope. The walls began to glow gold, the shadows more dark green than black. There was a sudden acrid smell like rotting vegetation, no, rotting seaweed. Albright continued to chant, his words, the light, the smell all combining to assail my senses. Confused, I stumbled against Archie. He put a protective arm around me but neither of us could move. I glanced towards the door in my panic, but I could not have crossed the room and left; my feet felt like lead.

Then I felt another presence enter the room. I sensed rather than saw something. The smell intensified and the shadows flickered as if someone were passing their hand in front of the lamp. One of the shadows detached and floated into the center of the circle, forming and reforming, sometimes in the shape of a man, then breaking up, diffusing and reforming into something indescribable. With each mutation it became more and more solid until it eventually resolved into a monster.

The creature stood like a man, being fully bipedal but with flippers like a frog's instead of hands. Its eyes bulged in the manner of The Drowned Man's but were even larger and more exaggerated. It seemed to be clothed in seaweed and it smelt like a midden. With a final, triumphant howl Albright seized me and dragged me into the circle. I was momentarily dizzy and fell on my knees. Albright grabbed my arm and used the merman's broken tail to cut it. This was not a scratch, as had activated the thing before but a bold slash that cut my arm almost from wrist to elbow. As my blood flowed onto the floor it formed into tiny beads that were taken up into the air and apparently incorporated into the monster.

The creature seemed to be feeding off me. Soon it seemed to me to fill the whole room. Its arms, if such they were, resembled fronds of seaweed and wrapped themselves tightly around my body. I struggled to breathe. Then, just when I felt as if all was up with me, two things happened very quickly. I could hear a voice, faint and far off. I realized it was Archie, outside the circle and chanting:

> "Ia, Dagon! Ia, Hydra! It is not yet time. I command your servant to depart from this place! Ia, Dagon! Ia, Hydra!"

The creature hesitated then recoiled as I felt sudden heat on my back. As it fell away I could see the same blue flame that had consumed Alice. There was an abominable smell like burning manure and the thing was gone. It had not been consumed by the fire, although it was undoubtedly damaged by it. It seemed like Archie's bizarre chanting had dismissed it.

Albright stood outside the circle rubbing his hands and smiling. It was not pleasant to see. "Capital!" he chuckled. "Absolutely splendid! And now, dear lady, you shall tell me how you did that. You would, perhaps, like a cup of tea? And he shuffled off back into the shop leaving a room full of foul-smelling steam and one very bemused lady behind him.

As soon as he'd gone I hissed to Archie "Was that magic? Since when can you do magic?" Archie shrugged. "I wouldn't call it magic as such. These things respond to certain words that carry some kind of force. It's like calling your dog; it doesn't know what the words mean; it just knows to get its ball or sit or something. Except dogs possess far greater intelligence than one of these things."

"What was it?" There was no time for Archie to answer as Albright had returned bearing a tray with a teapot, some rather chipped teacups with no saucers and, incongruously, a packet of digestive biscuits.

"Dig in, dig in!" he encouraged us. His attempt to smile looked like a wolf baring its teeth. "I say, this is capital! Utterly topping, as you young folk would say!" I had found Albright's usual dour demeanor sinister enough, but this *volte face* was even more disturbing.

Archie's eyes flashed. I could tell that he was having a great deal of difficulty in containing his temper.

"I have no wish to detain you further, Albright. You have demonstrated all too clearly what this thing can do. Miss Selcibuc, if you are ready", he took my arm and we walked towards the door. "I'll thank you to unlock that, Albright."

"But Miss Selcibuc hasn't had her tea," purred Albright. "What sort of gentleman would I be if I didn't offer a lady a cup of tea?"

"You are no kind of gentleman, Albright" snapped Archie. "In fact, I consider you a rank outsider!" He marched smartly to the door and put his hand over the lock. There was a loud snap and the door swung open.

Miss Selcibuc, if you would. I bid you good afternoon, Albright."

Albright assumed a mocking tone. "A good afternoon to you too, Glossop. And I think you'll find that we are all are outsiders".

Then we were out on Copenhagen Street Street on a lovely June afternoon.

"Archie, what in heaven's name happened in there?" I gasped.

"I think you'll find that heaven has very little to do with it, Neve old thing." Archie answered. "I will explain as best I can. For starters, I think we need tea. Tea and cake, in fact."

"Archie, I think Albright just tried to kill me. We don't need to go to a tea shop, we need to find a constable."

"I disagree, old thing. You need tea before we do anything. You'll feel better then, trust me."

As Archie had proved himself eminently reliable so far, I agreed to go to tea with him provided we got clear of Copenhagen Street. We found a place in Holborn and Archie ordered. Although it had only been an hour or so I realized that I was ravenously hungry and soon we were digging in to tea and scones.

Archie took a deep breath.

"I need to explain what has just happened", he said.

"Just a bit!" I agreed.

"Very well. Your little merman is, as you know, of great antiquity. It's almost certainly one of the artifacts found by Campbell Thompson in Nineveh. As a votive object it would have been kept in a household shrine and treated with the same veneration as a god. Nineveh eventually fell to the armies of its subject states but not everyone could flee. The invaders brought new ideas and most people grew to worship the gods of their new rulers but some continued to honor Dagon in secret.

Thousands of years of human thoughts and feelings, prayer energy, if you will, all stored up in this little object. A man could have buried it to protect his riches when the invaders arrived, or it might have been buried later, to hide it from non-believers or simply because no-one believed in the god any more. Then Thompson found it. It came back from Iraq – along with hundreds of other artifacts – but somehow got lost or stolen along the way. It's as likely it turned up in New York as anywhere else. Then your Drowned Man stole it and was bringing it to Blighty when it all went awry and the statue ended up with you, old thing."

"The Drowned Man took it and that's why he was on the liner?"

"That's right. I don't think he stole it for its monetary value, either. If that chap isn't one of Dagon's then I'm a Dutchman!" He thumped his fist on the table for emphasis. I plied the teapot and refilled both cups.

"That would also explain why he didn't drown. The God of the Waters protects his own. When he dropped that little merman – fishman is more accurate actually – he missed something that I picked up the very first time that I met you. Honoria did too. You have latent magical abilities. That's rare. And the first interaction you had with the fishman was to offer it a sacrifice, your blood. Even though that was unintentional it was enough to awaken it." He saw my surprise and gave me a tired smile.

"It is conscious, Neve. It is living, despite being forged in metal by a man thousands of years ago. The best explanation I can give is that it's a conduit to the god, to Dagon. He can connect with you from, I don't know, another dimension, perhaps. You offered him blood and he did something in return. He sent his holy fire down on those that displeased you."

Overcome with guilt, I confess that I started to cry. So I was responsible for the death of my cousin and of the antique dealer. I was a murderer.

"Alice was a goose and the dealer was a bounder but I didn't wish either of them any harm. I feel so bad."

He handed me a clean, freshly pressed handkerchief.

"Neve, you had no way of knowing. You didn't know you had magical ability never mind how to control it, to channel it. This really wasn't your fault. And you did just save both our lives."

"How so? What exactly happened in there?"

"Albright could see, as I did, that you were attuned to the object. So he summoned an entity – a demon, you might call it – to test his hypothesis. Dagon's will was greater than that of his servitor, so you won. Hence the blue fire. If your attunement wasn't strong, that thing would have killed you for certain and the warding Albright put around the circle would have killed me when I intervened, as I would have been honor-bound to do."

"Archie, are you a wizard?"

"I'm a ritual magician, Neve. So is Honoria". He sighed. "We haven't been entirely honest with you. You are our friend and we have the greatest affection for you, but we have also taken a professional interest, as you might say, since we met you at Boughton Court. Honoria twigged first of all that you had some talent and then you told me about the fishman. We were intrigued by you. Honoria was anxious to keep you near to her for your own protection and seized the opportunity to bring you to London although we were all sad at how that came about."

"And Alice?"

"About as magical as that teapot. But a more loyal, generous and affectionate friend you couldn't find anywhere. I have something to tell you. You finding that statue was no coincidence. In fact, I think it found you. Neve, where are your family from?"

"My mother is English. My father from New England."

Archie smiled. "I thought so. Neve, this might come as a bit of a shock, but I don't think you are entirely human."

It is a measure of my regard for Archie that I didn't slap his face right there and then.

"Dagon was never a major deity in Nineveh. You won't find him in any standard works on Mesopotamian religion. Dagon was a water deity and the few depictions we have of his worship show people with gills like the Drowned Man and, I'm afraid, big eyes like yours. It's many thousands of years since Nineveh was sacked and the people fled. In time, they bred with ordinary human beings and these, er, characteristics disappeared, or were softened at least. You've just kept the beautiful eyes.

"There's a war going on, Neve. These artifacts were stolen for a reason. We believe that unscrupulous people, occultists, plan to use some of them to summon an old god and bring down terrible tribulation on mankind. The Drowned Man was fighting them but only because he wants his god, Dagon, to return. He was prepared to sacrifice you, to destroy your immortal soul, Neve, to make that happen. Bingo and I didn't just protect you because you are our friend. We protected you because we have sworn a sacred oath that if this happened ..." He tailed off, choked with emotion.

"I think it's time for you to join us, Neve. We need to tutor you, to show you how to control that massive reservoir of power. And we need to take proper care of that fishman before someone else dies."

I didn't need to think about it. "Archie, I'd be honored. What now?"

" For now, I think it best that your little fishman remains with me, where he can't do any harm. This evening, my dear Sotor Neve, we must pay a brief visit to the Wentworth Club ."

Bingo, Honoria and I left Hampstead at twilight and drove into London, eventually parking outside a smart building in Mayfair, one of a number of private clubs in the area. The brass plate to the left of the door confirmed that we had reached our destination. Once inside, Honoria ushered me through to the Ladies Lounge.

"Welcome to the Wentworth Club, Neve," she smiled. "They've got some funny ideas about women but they're good old duffers really. Let me introduce you to some people then we'll have dinner and talk magic!"

The doings of the Wentworth Club are, I feel, rather too esoteric to commit to a diary that might easily be read by one's servants. I can say that I met some charming people tonight. I was especially excited to meet Theodore Rayburn-Price, who was happy to talk at length about antiquities and expeditions to far-off places/ We got on like a house on fire. There was also a chap called Aloysius Delgado who flirted quite outrageously with Honoria, much to Bingo's amusement. We left around midnight, Bingo speeding us back to Hampstead in the Crossley.

~ Tuesday 7th July ~

Today started with a telephone call from Archie. He was taking his first proper look at one of the boxes from Reginald Campbell Thompson's Nineveh dig. Would I like to join him? Would I! I was on the omnibus into town in a trice!

The items for examination were wrapped in felt and then packed in straw. Archie unwrapped each one in turn and I recorded his observations in a notebook. After a while, Archie put down a small golden animal and turned to me.

"Look Neve, there's something you should know. I asked you to come today so we could get this stuff cataloged in a hurry. I believe someone's stealing things from the Assyrian Gallery and I want you to help me. We need to keep accurate records of what we've got, certainly, but are you up for something rather more useful, and a great deal more exciting?"

"What are you suggesting?"

"We don't have enough evidence to call the police and if we're up against what I think we're up against then I don't want to get them involved. Taking good descriptions of these items is the first step. Thank you for your help with that. If there has been thieving, I think it's happened at night. The museum does have security, but they can't be everywhere at once. Will you stay here with me tonight in the Assyrian Gallery? I want to be here when those blighters come back. I swear they won't get a bally sausage while Archie Glossop's on patrol!"

It sounded like an adventure. Overnight in the British Museum in charming company. Of course I assented. A bell rang and Archie looked at his watch.

"Closing time. Let's get some air and come back in an hour. The museum staff should have left for the day by then."

As we made to leave the museum the professor supervising Archie's research hoved into view. Archie swore under his breath.

"Sorry old girl, but I have to go back to work. Could you take this?" Archie presented me with a small, heavy package. "I've drawn a blank but I know it's important and I know it didn't come from that original dig. Can you help me find out more about it?"

I sat on a bench in the grounds of the museum and carefully unwrapped the package. It was one of the felt-wrapped artifacts, a small, heavy statuette of a bearded man emerging from the body of another man. Unlike my little fishman this was obviously solid gold. It was no less disturbing. I had no idea what it was but I knew someone who probably did. I sighed. Time to visit Mr Albright.

My interview with Albright was conducted on a more equal footing on this occasion. He knew what I and my little fishman could do and did not try to provoke me in any way, although simply being in his presence made my flesh creep. He was extremely excited by the statue, repeating "Nabu, Nabu!" over and over. He muttered something under his breath about a chap called King, who I knew to have been directing the Nineveh excavations with Thompson. Putting together Albright's observations with what Archie had said earlier that day, it seemed that there had been a second dig and this statue was from it.

It must depict the god Nabu, who I knew to be the Assyrian deity of writing. Albright didn't want to discuss the matter further and in fact was keen to usher me out of the shop. He was pale and shaking and his demeanor terrified me. I was confused about why Archie had entrusted me with the statue of Nabu. How did he expect me to get more information? Then it occurred to me to hurry back to Honoria's and telephone my Uncle.

He was pleased to hear from me and reported that my Aunt was as well as could be expected, although the household was still in deep mourning. Bartram had been released without charge as the police were unable to extract any useful information from the woman. My consulting him on the matter of the statue would, he said, distract him from the dreadful events for a little while so he was happy to help me.

Half an hour later I had discovered that my Uncle had a great deal of knowledge in the matter of Assyrian mythology and he was able to explain the worship of Nabu in some detail. I scribbled the details of my visit to Albright on a picture postcard that I'd bought to send to my Mother and just caught the last post.

As I couldn't get back into the museum without Archie I abandoned the idea of a night time vigil and passed the evening with Honoria discussing the Wentworth Club. She filled me in on the details; who the important people were, Lord this and Lady that, all at top speed until I couldn't possibly take it all in. Bingo came home from his office and the evening ended quietly and quite early.

~ Wednesday 8th July ~

This afternoon brought a telephone call from Uncle Thomas. The postcard had arrived by second post and he was interested to read its contents. He suggested that I go to see Archie and that the three of us put our heads together, via the miracle of telephony, to see if we can between us establish the true significance of this statue. Something in his tone indicated that he would not be surprised by Archie's occult interpretations. As a friend of Albright's I imagine he had encountered items of this nature before.

It's three o'clock now. Just time to hurry to the museum and tell Archie that my Uncle is prepared to aid us in the matter of the statue.

6pm

My heart is broken. Archie, I promise on my life that I will find out who did this to you. You will have justice. Rest in Peace my best friend.

I am going to the Wentworth Club now. I have nowhere else to turn, and I will not bring dear Honoria or Bingo any deeper into this.